Argenta Press
Company's Coming

THE
Canadian Cowboy Cookbook
From the Ranch to the Backyard

Radford • Paré • Lepine

The Publisher: Argenta Press is an imprint of Dragon Hill Publishing Ltd.

Library and Archives Canada Cataloguing in Publication
Radford, Duane, 1946-, author
      The Canadian cowboy cookbook / Duane Radford, Jean Paré,
Gregory Lepine.
Includes index.
ISBN 978-1-77207-009-5 (pbk.)
      1. Cooking, Canadian. 2. Cowboys--Canada--Social life and customs.
3. Cookbooks. I. Paré, Jean, author II. Lepine, Gregory, author III. Title.
TX715.6.R3 2015   641.5971   C2015-901607-X

Cover Image: Cowboy silhouette © Sascha Burkard / Thinkstock; Leather texture © Danin Tulic / Thinkstock; Paper texture © Nastco / Thinkstock.

Produced with the assistance of the Government of Alberta,   *Alberta*
Alberta Media Fund.   Government

PC: 31

Distributed through
Company's Coming Publishing Limited

Table of Contents

Introduction

Cowboy cooking evolved during the historic American cattle drives from Texas to railheads in Kansas and Missouri after the Civil War ended in 1865. Cowboy cooking spread to Canada with the development of the ranching industry of western Canada in the days after the North-West Mounted Police marched west in 1874. The Mounties needed food, and a few entrepreneurs saw an opportunity in driving cattle up from Montana to establish herds near the police forts. The heyday of the Canadian cowboy lasted into the 1920s but the myth of the cowboy continues to this day.

The Spanish influence on cowboy recipes was huge in the southern United States, particularly in Arizona, Colorado, Texas, New Mexico, Nevada and California, and was the genesis of many spicy recipes that remain popular to this day. In Canada and many mid-western and north-western states, cowboy recipes tended to be influenced by the British, Scottish and Irish origins of the cowboys. Many recipes in this book feature those origins, although other European influences can also be identified in some recipes.

Range etiquette during the historic cattle drives was simple: the camp cook ruled the roost. He kept a strict eye on his chuckwagon, where all his ingredients were stored and where most of the food was prepared, and the area around it including the fire. Woe to the cowboy who offended him or who violated that sacred ground until being summoned for a meal by the dinner bell. Most of the chuckwagon cooks in the early days were men; stories abound of their colourful nature and their primitive working conditions.

Cowboys burned up a lot of calories while working, consequently meals tended to be hearty. The cattle drive became a seasonal event as time went by; but daily chores such as rounding up cattle, building and repairing fences, cutting hay, pitching bales and watering cattle were are all hard work, done in the outdoors often during inclement weather. Historic photos depict cowboys as being lean, a testament to a hard day's work on an ongoing basis. Working cowboys also tended to miss meals while out on the range chasing a stray dogie.

Main dishes for cowboys recipes featured chicken, beef and pork done up as casseroles, stews, as well as being fried and roasted. Ground meat featured prominently in the diet of ranchers, as burgers, meat balls, in casseroles such as shepherd's pies and in stews. About half of a heifer would end up as ground meat, and/or trim for sausages. Many ranchers

of European descent would use beef trim to make garlic sausage, always a popular treat. There were also recipes for barbecued ribs from both cattle and pigs; most often they would be boiled for various lengths of time prior to being barbecued or roasted in a Dutch oven, seasoned with various spices and sauces. A wide variety of baked bean recipes using kidney, navy and pinto beans were often a mainstay on long cattle drives and made their way into subsequent generations of favourites.

Many seasonings could readily be found in the isolated ranch kitchens. If there's one thing country cooks disdain, it would be complicated recipes with hard-to-find (and seldom used) seasonings. Common seasonings included basil, chili powder, cinnamon, cloves, nutmeg, oregano, paprika, thyme, bay leaf and pickling spices. Dry mustard, white vinegar, molasses, brown and white sugar were also staples in a ranch kitchen, as well as Worcestershire sauce, a popular sauce that has been around since the mid-1800s, and hot sauces such as Tabasco sauce, also available since the late 1800s.

Cowboy cooking almost invariably included a lot of wild game recipes: waterfowl, grouse and partridge, as well as pronghorn and venison cooked in a great many ways. Wild game tends to be quite lean, so it was often braised, cooked in Dutch ovens or made into stews and casseroles to keep the meat moist.

Salads were made from fruits, asparagus, broccoli, corn, cucumbers, peas, beets, potatoes, tomatoes and lettuce. Coleslaw has always been part of the western ranch heritage. Cabbage would also be made into cabbage rolls and sauerkraut. Sauerkraut and spare ribs were often favourites, as many ranch families were of European origin. Beets would be made into borscht and pickled beets.

Wild berries such as saskatoons, blueberries, strawberries and raspberries were used in pancakes, cakes, muffins and pies. Saskatoons and choke-cherries were also made into jams, jellies and syrup.

Cowboys have a sweet tooth, as evidenced by a great many recipes for cookies, candy, pies and cakes. Apples often were the key ingredient in desserts such as apple cobbler, apple crisp, apple sauce cake and apple pie.

Cowboy recipes tended to feature a rather short list of fairly common ingredients. In the early days, most of the products were home grown; a large garden could make the difference between getting through the winter or not.

Various methods of preservation were used to store meat and vegetables. For example, parts of the head of a calf or pig would be made into head cheese, a meat jelly that could be stored in the pantry for use as a cold cut. Many vegetables were preserved by canning, or stored in root cellars during the winter. Leftover food often ended up in soup; consequently, cooks would adapt their recipes as they went along depending on what was on hand. Scraps went into slop or compost.

The cowboy tradition of cooking has made an enduring contribution to Canadian cuisine. Women eventually joined the chuckwagon cook in meal preparation in the kitchens of the farms and ranches that were established as time went on, and they carried cowboy cooking through the generations.

Cowboy Breakfast

Nothing beats a casserole, regardless of the season, and this easy-to-make cowboy breakfast is a keeper. The mouth-watering ingredients are sure to satisfy almost any palate and are made even more appealing with the addition of bacon drippings and fried bacon slices. Cowboy breakfasts tend to be high on calories to supply the energy the cowboys need to tackle a long day of farm and ranch chores.

Bacon slices, diced	6	6
Chopped green pepper	1/4 cup	60 mL
Chopped onion	1/4 cup	60 mL
Frozen hash brown potatoes, thawed	2 cups	500 mL
Large eggs	4	4
Water	1/4 cup	60 mL
Salt	1/2 tsp.	2 mL
Pepper	1/8 tsp.	0.5 mL
Grated medium Cheddar cheese	1/2 cup	125 mL
Grated part-skim mozzarella cheese	1/2 cup	125 mL
Chopped fresh parsley, for garnish		

Combine first 3 ingredients in a large non-stick frying pan on medium. Cook for 5 to 10 minutes, stirring often, until bacon is crisp. Remove with slotted spoon to paper towel to drain. Drain all but 1 tbsp. (15 mL) drippings from pan.

Press hash browns evenly in same frying pan. Cook, uncovered, for about 10 minutes on medium-low, stirring occasionally, until crisp.

Beat next 4 ingredients in a small bowl. Stir in bacon mixture. Pour over hash browns.

Sprinkle with half of Cheddar and mozzarella. Cook for about 5 minutes, stirring occasionally, until almost set. Turn oven to broil with rack in middle. Remove casserole from pan and place in an 8 x 8 inch (20 x 20 cm) baking dish. Sprinkle with remaining cheese and broil for 5 minutes. Garnish with parsley. Serves 4.

1 serving: 600 Calories; 46 g Total Fat (19 g Mono, 4.5 g Poly, 18 g Sat); 275 mg Cholesterol; 25 g Carbohydrate (2 g Fibre, 2 g Sugar); 21 g Protein); 1030 mg Sodium

*If you climb in the saddle,
be ready for the ride.*

Scrambled Breakfast

Eggs were not often available on the trail, but they were a fixture on farms and ranches. A hearty scrambled breakfast would be a favourite meal for cowboys before a day's work on the range. Folks in a hurry will appreciate this omelette that's as easy to make as falling off a log. The aroma will draw a crowd around the breakfast table.

Large eggs	8	8
Water	2 tbsp.	30 mL
Salt	1/2 tsp.	2 mL
Pepper	1/4 tsp.	1 mL
Cooking oil	1 tbsp.	15 mL
Chopped onion	1 cup	250 mL
Sliced fresh white mushrooms	2 cups	500 mL
Chopped ham (or bacon)	1 cup	250 mL

Whisk first 4 ingredients in a medium bowl until frothy.

Heat cooking oil in a large frying pan on medium-high. Add onion and mushrooms. Cook for 8 to 10 minutes, stirring often, until onion is soft and golden.

Add ham and cook, stirring, for about 2 minutes until ham is starting to turn brown. Reduce heat to medium. Add egg mixture. Cook, stirring, for about 4 minutes until eggs are set but not dry. Serves 4.

1 serving: 260 Calories; 17 g Total Fat (7 g Mono, 3 g Poly, 4.5 g Sat); 445 mg Cholesterol; 6 g Carbohydrate (1 g Fibre, 3 g Sugar); 22 g Protein; 960 mg Sodium

You can always tell a cowboy, but you can't tell him much.

Spinach and Bacon Omelette

Cured meat, especially bacon, was a staple in the cowboy diet. The use of Canadian bacon in this omelette gives it a back-country dimension, while the combination of spinach, bacon, mushrooms and Cheddar cheese will satisfy even a gourmet's palate. Cowboys would be keen on getting some green in their diets, and spinach would be a natural choice.

Butter (or hard margarine)	3 tsp.	15 mL
Sliced fresh white mushrooms	1/2 cup	125 mL
Back (Canadian) bacon slices, cut into thin strips	1/2 oz.	14 g
Thinly sliced green onion	1/3 cup	75 mL
Fresh spinach leaves, lightly packed	1 cup	250 mL
Large eggs	3	3
Milk	1 tbsp.	15 mL
Salt, to taste		
Pepper, to taste		
Butter (or hard margarine)	1 tsp.	5 mL
Grated light medium Cheddar cheese	2 tbsp.	30 mL

Melt first amount of butter in a medium non-stick frying pan on medium. Add next 3 ingredients. Cook for 2 to 3 minutes, stirring occasionally, until mushrooms are softened.

Add spinach. Cook, stirring, for about 1 minute until spinach is wilted and liquid is almost evaporated. Transfer to a small bowl. Set aside.

Whisk next 4 ingredients in a separate small bowl until smooth.

Melt second amount of butter in same frying pan on medium. Tilt pan as butter melts until bottom is coated. Pour egg mixture into pan. Reduce heat to medium-low. When starting to set at outside edge, tilt pan and gently lift cooked egg mixture with spatula, easing around pan from outside edge in. Allow uncooked egg mixture to flow onto bottom of pan. Repeat, working around pan, until egg is softly set.

Sprinkle cheese and spinach mixture over half of omelette. Fold other half of omelette over spinach mixture. Cook, covered, for about 2 minutes until cheese is melted. Serves 2.

1 serving: 220 Calories; 17 g Total Fat (5 g Mono, 4.5 g Poly, 8 g Sat); 350 mg Cholesterol; 4 g Carbohydrate (trace Fibre, 2 g Sugar); 14 g Protein; 320 mg Sodium

Very tasty.
Used pineapple
bacon
and brocolli
Bitty doesn't like
pineapple etc
Plain omelette!

Corned Beef Hash and Eggs

Corned beef hash is an old standby cowboy recipe that dates back to 19th-century cattle drives in the United States. It was, and still is, a favourite on farms and ranches, as well as among outdoorsmen in Canada. This tasty meal really sticks to the ribs and satisfies the appetite of folks engaged in demanding physical activities. Among cowboys, it has long had universal appeal.

Diced cooked peeled potato (about 1/4 inch, 6 mm pieces)	2 cups	500 mL
Cooked corned beef, cut into chunks	1 lb.	454 g
Finely chopped onion	1/2 cup	125 mL
Milk	1 1/2 tbsp.	22 mL
Pepper	1/4 tsp.	1 mL
Butter (or hard margarine)	1 tbsp.	15 mL
Large eggs	4	4
Chopped fresh parsley	3 tbsp.	45 mL
Salt, to taste		

Combine first 5 ingredients in a medium bowl.

Melt butter in a frying pan on medium-low. Stir in corned beef mixture. Cook, covered, for about 15 minutes, stirring occasionally, until heated through. Cook, uncovered, for about 35 minutes, stirring occasionally, until browned.

Make 4 holes in hash and break 1 egg into each. Cook, covered, over moderately low heat for 5 minutes, or until eggs are cooked to desired doneness. Sprinkle with parsley and salt. Serves 4.

1 serving: 570 Calories; 38 g Total Fat (17 g Mono, 2.5 g Poly, 14 g Sat); 330 mg Cholesterol; 25 g Carbohydrate (2 g Fibre, 3 g Sugar); 30 g Protein; 1390 mg Sodium

Spiced Sweet Potato Hash

Potato hash comes in many forms—typically as a side dish with bacon or sausages and eggs—and has long been a favourite of cooks who need to use up potatoes left over from earlier meals. It can, however, be a meal in itself, as in this recipe, which features sweet potatoes as the main ingredient. The chili and paprika seasoning sets this recipe apart and brings out the flavour in the potatoes.

Cooking oil	1 tsp.	5 mL
Sausage, chopped	1 cup	250 mL
Cooking oil	2 tbsp.	30 mL
Cubed, peeled orange-fleshed sweet potato	3 cups	750 mL
Chopped green onion	1/2 cup	125 mL
Chopped red pepper	1/2 cup	125 mL
Chili powder	1/2 tsp.	2 mL
Paprika	1/2 tsp.	2 mL
Salt	1/2 tsp.	2 mL
Pepper	1/2 tsp.	2 mL
Ground cinnamon	1/8 tsp.	0.5 mL

Heat first amount of cooking oil in a medium frying pan on medium-high. Add sausage. Cook, stirring, for about 5 minutes, until sausage starts to brown. Remove from pan and set aside.

Heat second amount of cooking oil in pan on medium-high. Add sweet potato. Cook, stirring, for about 5 minutes until starting to brown. Reduce heat to medium-low.

Stir in remaining 7 ingredients. Cook, covered, for about 5 minutes, stirring occasionally, until sweet potato is tender. Serves 4.

1 serving: 300 Calories; 20 g Total Fat (11 g Mono, 4 g Poly, 5 g Sat); 30 mg Cholesterol; 24 g Carbohydrate (4 g Fibre, 5 g Sugar); 7 g Protein; 650 mg Sodium

Molasses Porridge

Porridge has deep roots in Canadian history—it was often a fixture for cowboys who rode for the brand and would have been standard fare for chuckwagon cooks, as well as on farms and ranches back in the day. It was also a popular breakfast item among pioneer settlers, particularly those of British descent, especially on cold mornings. A cowboy would almost automatically have topped his porridge with a spoonful or two of molasses to sweeten things up a bit. This recipe, however, raises the bar even higher with the addition of some tasty nutmeg and fresh berries.

Water	2 1/4 cups	550 mL
Apple juice	1 cup	250 mL
Salt	1/4 tsp.	1 mL
Old-fashioned rolled oats	2 cups	250 mL
Ground nutmeg	1 tsp.	5 mL
Molasses	3 tbsp.	45 mL
Sliced strawberries	1/2 cup	125 mL
Raspberries	1/4 cup	60 mL
Blueberries	1/4 cup	60 mL
Milk (optional)	1 cup	250 mL

Bring water, apple juice and salt to a boil in a medium saucepan.

Combine rolled oats and nutmeg in a small bowl and add to saucepan. Reduce heat to a simmer and cook for 5 minutes, uncovered, stirring occasionally.

Remove pan from heat and stir in molasses. Let sit for 2 minutes, covered.

Mix berries in a medium bowl. Divide porridge among 4 bowls and top with berry mixture and milk, if using. Serves 4.

1 serving: 240 Calories; 3.5 g Total Fat (1 g Mono, 1 g Poly, 0 g Sat); 0 mg Cholesterol; 50 g Carbohydrate (5 g Fibre, 20 g Sugar); 5 g Protein; 170 mg Sodium

Red River cereal is a Canadian brand of hot cereal that originated in Manitoba's Red River Valley in the 1920s. It is a mixture of cracked wheat, cracked rye and flax and has a mild nutty flavour.

God does not hold men accountable for the cussing done at cows.

Wild Blueberry Maple Pancakes

This recipe showcases ingredients that are classic Canadiana. Grilled pancakes studded with wild blueberries are topped with crushed blueberries infused with maple syrup. Fresh fruit was a welcome treat in the cowboy diet, and a cowboy that brought berries back to the chuckwagon won some brownie points with the cook, and with the other cowboys. Saskatoon berries would have been one of the most common berries cowboys encountered, with blueberries growing north of the traditional cowboy range, but we find the lure of blueberry pancakes irresistible. Feel free to substitute other berries if you'd prefer a more authentic cowboy pancake.

Maple syrup	2 tbsp.	30 mL
Wild blueberries (see Tip, below)	1 cups	250 mL
Flour	1 cup	250 mL
Baking powder	1 tsp.	5 mL
Baking soda	1/2 tsp.	2 mL
Milk	1 cup	250 mL
Large egg, beaten	1	1
Melted butter	2 tbsp.	30 mL
Maple syrup	2 tbsp.	30 mL
Blueberries	1 cup	250 mL

In a small pot, heat first amount of maple syrup until just warm. Add first amount of blueberries to syrup and mash. Heat syrup and blueberries until mixture just starts to boil. Remove from heat and set aside.

In a medium bowl, combine flour, baking powder and baking soda and mix well.

In a separate bowl, combine milk, egg, butter, second amount of maple syrup and second amount of blueberries. Pour into dry ingredients and mix well. Preheat grill to medium. In a frying pan or greased skillet, pour 1/4 cup (60 mL) batter. When deep holes or bubbles appear in pancake, flip over and cook other side. Repeat for each pancake. Serve with blueberry syrup. Serves 4.

1 serving: 290 Calories; 8 g Total Fat (2 g Mono, 0.5 g Poly, 2.5 g Sat); 70 mg Cholesterol; 48 g Carbohydrate (3 g Fibre, 20 g Sugar); 8 g Protein; 330 mg Sodium

Tip: Blueberries can be frozen and used at any time of the year, provided they're dry and not packed together too tightly.

 Cowboys may not have been too particular about what they ate, but they would not go without coffee. Cowboy coffee was notoriously strong, "strong enough to float a horseshoe," according to cowboy lore. The rule of thumb was a handful of grounds per cup of water. Because there were no filters, the coffee grounds were boiled with egg shells, which would make the grounds sink to the bottom of the pot. A chuckwagon cook worth his pay would always have a pot brewing over the fire. Cowboys on the range, who did not have access to a chuckwagon, brewed "sock coffee"—they filled a (hopefully clean) sock with grounds and boiled it.

Pancake Breakfasts

🌾 In North America, the terms "pancake" and "flapjack" are synonymous, but in the UK, flapjacks are sweet bars made of butter, oats and corn syrup.

Pancakes and the iconic image most folks have of cowboys just don't seem to jive at first glance. Odd as it may sound, however, pancakes, of all things, are synonymous with cowboys and cowboy culture. They're more or less a western institution, probably because they are easy to make, use common ingredients, can be tailor made with local ingredients to match a person's particular tastes, plus they are filling. They have long been a breakfast staple on farms and ranches throughout the West.

In her book *Come 'n' Get It* (1966), B.M. Barss writes that cowboys and chuckwagon cooks did not follow a written recipe for pancakes. Instead, they followed a rule of thumb and used 1:1 proportions for each ingredient: that is, 1 cup flour, 1 cup liquid, 1 egg, 1 rounded teaspoon baking powder, 1 teaspoon melted fat or drippings and 1 pinch of salt. The batter was added to a greased skillet; then, after bubbles formed, it was flipped over once and cooked on the other side. The proportion of ingredients may have changed somewhat over time, but the love of this breakfast staple has not.

From this appreciation for pancakes grew one of the Calgary Stampede's most famous and beloved traditions, the Stampede pancake breakfast. According to Calgary Stampede records, the first free Stampede breakfast was held in 1923 at a campsite just outside the Canadian Pacific Railway station close to downtown Calgary. Apparently Jack Morton, a chuckwagon driver, invited some friends to join him for breakfast at his camp. People who wandered by as the group was eating were invited to share the pancake breakfast, and a tradition was born that continues to this day. There are many free Calgary Stampede pancake breakfasts during the 10-day event (each morning except on parade day), which are hosted by various groups throughout the city. They feature pancakes, of course, as well as piping hot coffee and usually bacon or sausages, a tribute to the city's hallmark western hospitality. Visiting dignitaries and politicians are often pressed into flipping pancakes at these events.

Thanks to the popularity of the Stampede breakfast, the event has grown into something of a national institution. Communities throughout Canada put on pancake breakfasts to celebrate special events, from national holidays like Canada Day to small local festivities, or as fundraisers. The tradition has even trickled into the United States, all thanks to a generous man who was willing to share his breakfast with a group of strangers.

Goulash Soup

A goulash is a Hungarian soup or stew made with a variety of meat and vegetables, seasoned with paprika. It is sometimes called Esterhazy goulash to honour the Esterhazy family in historic Hungarian nobility. The word "goulash" comes from the Hungarian guylás, *meaning "herdsman." The stew was popular among herdsman on the Hungarian plains because all the ingredients, including wild vegetables such as onion, were easily found. It also became a staple in the Canadian West, introduced by Hungarian homesteaders, and would have no doubt been part of a chuckwagon cook's repertoire.*

All-purpose flour	2 tbsp.	30 mL
Paprika *sub*	1 tsp.	5 mL
Pepper	1/2 tsp.	2 mL
Stewing beef, trimmed of fat, cut into 1 inch (2.5 cm) cubes	1 lb.	454 g
Cooking oil	1 tbsp.	15 mL
Chopped onion	1 cup	250 mL
Water	1/4 cup	60 mL
Garlic clove, minced	1	1
Beef stock	4 cups	1 L
Caraway seed	1 tsp.	5 mL
Can of diced tomatoes (14 oz., 398 mL), with juice	1	1
Diced carrot	1 cup	250 mL
Diced yellow turnip	1 cup	250 mL
Diced peeled potato	1 cup	250 mL

Measure first 3 ingredients into a large resealable plastic bag. Add beef, seal bag and toss until coated.

Heat cooking oil in a large saucepan on medium-high. Add beef. Cook, stirring, for 3 to 4 minutes until browned. Reduce heat to medium.

Add next 3 ingredients. Cook for about 5 to 10 minutes, scraping any brown bits from bottom of pan, until onion starts to soften.

Add stock and caraway seed. Bring to a boil. Reduce heat to medium-low. Simmer, partially covered, for about 45 minutes, stirring occasionally, until beef is tender.

Add remaining 4 ingredients. Bring to a boil. Cook, partially covered, for about 30 minutes, stirring occasionally, until vegetables are tender. Serves 4.

1 serving: 330 Calories; 12 g Total Fat (5 g Mono, 1.5 g Poly, 3 g Sat); 55 mg Cholesterol; 26 g Carbohydrate (3 g Fibre, 9 g Sugar); 30 g Protein; 1120 mg Sodium

Tex-Mex Hamburger Soup

This tangy recipe has its roots in the Spanish vaquero (i.e., cowboy) history of the southwestern United States and features traditional Mexican ingredients such as kidney beans, peppers, salsa and Monterey Jack cheese. Monterey Jack (or "Jack") cheese originated in Monterey, California. It's a pale yellow cheese first made by Mexican friars. This soup tastes even better the next day.

Cooking oil	2 tsp.	10 mL
Lean ground beef	1 lb.	454 g
Beef stock	6 cups	1.5 L
Can of kidney beans (19 oz., 540 mL), rinsed and drained	1	1
Chopped red onion	2 cups	500 mL
Can of diced tomatoes (14 oz., 398 mL), with juice	1	1
Chopped celery	1 1/2 cups	375 mL
Grated carrot	1 1/2 cups	375 mL
Chopped green pepper	1 cup	250 mL
Chunky salsa	1 cup	250 mL
Brown sugar, packed	1 tsp.	5 mL
Dried basil	1 tsp.	5 mL
Chopped fresh parsley (or 3/4 tsp., 4 mL, flakes)	1 tbsp.	15 mL
Sour cream	1/2 cup	125 mL
Grated Monterey Jack cheese	1/2 cup	125 mL

Heat cooking oil in a large frying pan on medium. Add beef and scramble-fry for about 10 minutes, until no longer pink. Drain well. Transfer to a slow cooker or Dutch oven.

Stir in next 10 ingredients. Cook, covered, on Low for 8 to 10 hours or on High for 4 to 5 hours for a slow cooker or in a 325°F (160° C) oven for 2 to 2 1/2 hours for a Dutch oven, until vegetables are tender.

Stir in parsley. Top individual servings with a dollop of sour cream and a sprinkle of cheese. Serves 7.

1 serving: 357 Calories; 15 g Total Fat (5 g Mono, 0.5 g Poly, 7 g Sat); 55 mg Cholesterol; 26 g Carbohydrate (8 g Fibre, 10 g Sugar); 22 g Protein; 1290 mg Sodium

Campfire Soup

It's no secret that cowboys enjoy beef: steaks with their breakfast, ground beef in chili with dinner, cubed beef in soup for supper. This dish most likely got its start when a camp cook, preparing the evening meal in a cast iron Dutch oven over a campfire, decided to add some diced leftover steak to his soup to give it some added consistency. The result is a thick, hearty soup that would satisfy even the hungriest cowboy.

Cooking oil	2 tsp.	10 mL
Beef top sirloin steak, trimmed of fat and diced	1 lb.	454 g
Chopped onion	1 cup	250 mL
Garlic cloves, minced (or 1/2 tsp., 2 mL, powder)	2	2
Beef stock	5 cups	1.25 L
Cubed, peeled potato	2 cups	500 mL
Baby carrots, halved	1 cup	250 mL
Tomato paste	1 tbsp.	15 mL
Worcestershire sauce	1 tbsp.	15 mL
Dried thyme	1/4 tsp.	1 mL
Salt	1/4 tsp.	1 mL
Water	1/4 cup	60 mL
All-purpose flour	1/4 cup	60 mL
Frozen peas	1 cup	250 mL

Heat cooking oil in a large saucepan on medium-high. Add beef and cook for about 10 minutes, stirring often, until browned.

Reduce heat to medium. Add onion and garlic. Cook for 3 to 5 minutes, stirring occasionally, until onion is softened.

Stir in stock and bring to a boil. Reduce heat to medium-low. Simmer, partially covered, for about 40 minutes until beef is tender.

Add next 6 ingredients. Bring to a boil.

Stir water into flour in a small bowl until smooth. Slowly add to soup, stirring constantly, until boiling and thickened. Reduce heat to medium. Boil gently, covered, for 15 to 20 minutes, stirring occasionally, until vegetables are tender.

Add peas. Cook, stirring, for 3 to 5 minutes until peas are tender. Serves 6.

1 serving: 290 Calories; 13 g Total Fat (6 g Mono, 1 g Poly, 4.5 g Sat); 50 mg Cholesterol; 23 g Carbohydrate (3 g Fibre, 6 g Sugar); 20 g Protein; 810 mg Sodium

Chuckwagon Stew

Chuckwagon stew is a throwback to the days of early cattle drives where just about anything might end up in the stew pot, from brains to choice cuts of meat. Such a stew brings back fond memories of cowboys chowing down around a campfire on the plains after a day on the trail. Fresh ingredients were few and far between for cowboys on the trail, but a good chuckwagon cook would load his wagon with non-perishable items like canned tomatoes and spices before setting out, so he could offer the crew a little variety to what could otherwise be a pretty bland diet.

Chopped onion	1/2 cup	125mL
Cooking oil	1 tbsp.	15 mL
All-purpose flour	2 tbsp.	30 mL
Boneless beef inside round (or blade or chuck) steak, trimmed of fat and cubed	3/4 lb.	340 g
Water	4 cups	1 L
Medium potatoes, diced	4	4
Can of diced tomatoes (14 oz., 398 mL), with juice	1	1
Frozen kernel corn	1/2 cup	125 mL
Paprika	1/2 tsp.	2 mL
Sugar	1/2 tsp.	2 mL
Salt	1 tsp.	5 mL
Pepper	1/4 tsp.	1 mL

(handwritten: chuck)

Sauté onion in cooking oil in a large pot or Dutch oven until soft and golden. Stir in flour until well mixed. Turn into a small bowl and set aside.

Put beef and water into same pot. Simmer, covered for 1 to 1 1/2 hours until tender.

Add next 7 ingredients. Cook for 25 minutes. Add reserved onion mixture. Cook, stirring, until boiling and thickened. Serves 6.

1 serving: 300 Calories; 12 g Total Fat (6 g Mono, 1 g Poly, 4 g Sat); 40 mg Cholesterol; 34 g Carbohydrate (3 g Fibre, 5 g Sugar); 14 g Protein; 650 mg Sodium

Get small can tom.
Allow 1-2 Hrs to create
Red onion?
Made April 1/16

Round-up Stew

Rich and hearty, this stew would be the perfect way to top off a long day in the saddle, rounding up cattle. We like to think of it as a modern version of Son-of-a-bitch (or "Son-of-a-gun" in polite company) Stew, which was a common meal for cowboys in the past but is probably an acquired taste, not likely to appeal to modern sensibilities. When a cow was slaughtered, cooks made that infamous stew to use up the less choice bits. Recipes differed, but common ingredients included brains, tongue, liver, heart and sweetbreads. Basically, according to author Ramon Adams, the cook would "throw everything in the pot but the horns and hide."

Cooking oil	2 tsp.	10 mL
Extra-lean ground beef	1/2 lb.	225 g
Sliced fresh white mushrooms	1/2 cup	125 mL
Chopped onion	1/2 cup	125 mL
Chopped celery	1/2 cup	125 mL
All-purpose flour	2 tsp.	10 mL
Beef stock	6 cups	1.5 L
Sliced carrot	1 cup	250 mL
Chopped peeled potato	1 cup	250 mL
Pearl barley	1/3 cup	75 mL
Tomato paste	2 tbsp.	30 mL
Pepper	1/4 tsp.	1 mL
Can of evaporated milk (5 1/2 oz., 160 mL)	1	1

Heat cooking oil in a large saucepan on medium. Add next 4 ingredients. Scramble-fry for about 10 minutes until beef is no longer pink.

Sprinkle with flour. Cook, stirring, for 1 minute.

Add next 6 ingredients. Bring to a boil. Reduce heat to medium-low. Simmer, partially covered, for about 1 hour, stirring occasionally, until barley and vegetables are tender and stew is thickened.

Add evaporated milk. Cook, stirring, for 1 to 2 minutes until heated through. Serves 4.

1 serving: 280 Calories; 7 g Total Fat (3.5 g Mono, 1 g Poly, 2 g Sat); 30 mg Cholesterol; 34 g Carbohydrate (4 g Fibre, 11 g Sugar); 21 g Protein; 1180 mg Sodium

Hearty Chuckwagon Chili

Chili is synonymous with cowboy cuisine. You can't go wrong with chili, which is a family favourite at any time of the year, and is easy to make. This recipe has some added heat from the diced green chilies, offset somewhat by the cumin. It is the perfect dish for a backyard cookout but can also be made inside on the stovetop if more rustic cooking is not your style. Serve with biscuits or cornbread for an authentic cowboy meal.

Lean ground beef *chicken*	1 lb.	454 g
Chopped onion	1 cup	250 mL
Garlic cloves, finely chopped	2	2
Chunky salsa	2 1/2 cups	625 mL
Can of diced green chilies (4 oz., 114 mL)	1	1
Chili powder	2 tsp.	10 mL
Ground cumin	1/2 tsp.	2 mL
Cans of red kidney beans (14 oz., 398 mL), rinsed and drained	2	2

Prepare campfire. In a Dutch oven, sauté ground beef, onion and garlic until nicely browned. Drain off fat. Stir in salsa, chilies, chili powder and cumin. Stir in kidney beans and bring to a boil. Move Dutch oven farther away from fire to reduce heat to low and cover. Cook for about 30 minutes. Serves 6.

1 serving: 280 Calories; 11 g Total Fat (4.5 g Mono, 0 g Poly, 4 g Sat); 45 mg Cholesterol; 19 g Carbohydrate (6 g Fibre, 8 g Sugar); 19 g Protein; 930 mg Sodium

Only a fool argues with a skunk, a mule or a cook.

Barbecue Baked Beans √

Baked beans have long been a staple of country fare and back in the day were a mainstay of Texas cattle drives. Top of mind are visions of cowboys sitting beside their saddle with a plate of beans. Nowadays, they're often a meal in themselves, always a treat on farms and ranches. The secret is to cook the beans at a low heat for a relatively long time and ensure they've been soaked overnight before starting the slow-cooking process. They can be served alone with thick slices of freshly baked bread topped with mounds of butter, or as a side dish with roast beef, steaks or ribs. The chili sauce and Dijon mustard give this recipe just a bit of delectable heat.

Dried navy beans	2 cups	500 mL
Water	6 cups	1.5 L
Water	2 1/2 cups	625 mL
Cooking oil	1 tsp.	5 mL
Chopped onion	1 cup	250 mL
Garlic cloves, minced (or 1/2 tsp., 2 mL, powder)	2	2
Can of tomato sauce (14 oz., 398 mL)	1	1
Brown sugar, packed	1/3 cup	75 mL
Apple cider vinegar	1/4 cup	60 mL
Diced cooked bacon	1/4 cup	60 mL
Chili sauce	1/4 cup	60 mL
Dijon mustard	1 tbsp.	15 mL
Worcestershire sauce	1 tbsp.	15 mL
Salt	1 tsp.	5 mL
Pepper	1/2 tsp.	2 mL

Put beans into a large bowl. Add first amount of water. Let stand, covered, for at least 8 hours or overnight. Drain and rinse beans.

Put beans and second amount of water into a slow cooker or Dutch oven.

Heat cooking oil in a small frying pan on medium. Add onion and garlic. Cook for 5 to 10 minutes, stirring occasionally, until onion is softened. Add to beans. Cook, covered, on Low for 7 to 8 hours or on High for 3 1/2 to 4 hours for a slow cooker, or in a 350°F (160°C) oven for 1 1/2 to 2 hours for a Dutch oven.

Combine remaining 9 ingredients in a small bowl. Add to slow cooker or Dutch oven. Stir. Cook, covered, on High for 1 hour in slow cooker, or in oven for 30 minutes for Dutch oven. Serves 7.

1 serving: 340 Calories; 7 g Total Fat (2.5 g Mono, 1.5 g Poly, 2 g Sat); 5 mg Cholesterol; 56 g Carbohydrate (11 g Fibre, 18 g Sugar); 16 g Protein; 920 mg Sodium

To cook this dish outdoors in a cast iron or aluminum Dutch oven, place 9 briquettes under its base and 15 on the lid.

Whisky Baked Beans

Cowboy wisdom: "Whisky—the reason I wake up every afternoon." In cowboy folklore whisky is seemingly inseparable from cowboys, so it seems inevitable that it would have found its way into a baked beans recipe. Bourbon is a corn-based whisky aged in oak barrels, and along with the hickory sauce, it imparts a rich flavour to the baked beans.

Bourbon whisky	1/4 cup	60 mL
Hickory barbecue sauce	1/4 cup	60 mL
Maple syrup	1/4 cup	60 mL
Apple cider vinegar	1 tbsp.	15 mL
Dry mustard	1 tbsp.	15 mL
Salt	1/4 tsp.	1 mL
Pepper	1/4 tsp.	1 mL
Cans of navy beans (19 oz., 540 mL), rinsed and drained	2	2
Can of diced tomatoes (14 oz., 398 mL), with juice	1	1
Finely chopped onion	1 cup	250 mL

Combine first 7 ingredients in a large bowl.

Stir in remaining 3 ingredients. Transfer to an ungreased 2 quart (2 L) casserole. Bake, covered, in 375°F (190°C) oven for 1 hour. Bake, uncovered, for about 10 minutes until sauce is thickened. Serves 5.

1 serving: 150 Calories; 0 g Total Fat (0 g Mono, 0 g Poly, 0 g Sat); 0 mg Cholesterol; 26 g Carbohydrate (5 g Fibre, 1 g Sugar); 4 g Protein; 650 mg Sodium

In Canada navy beans had top billing with chuckwagon and ranch cooks, but in the south, pinto and vaquero beans are more common. The vaquero is a mild-flavoured black and white heirloom bean. As it cooks, it turns the surrounding liquid a rich, deep brownish black colour.

To cook this dish outdoors in a cast iron or aluminum Dutch oven, place 11 briquettes under its base and 17 on the lid.

Salsa Bean Cakes

Okay, so this isn't a baked bean recipe, but traditionally it would have been made from leftover baked beans, so we think it still qualifies. This recipe is a tip of the hat to the vaqueros—the original cowboys who tended cattle herds in Mexico that were brought to the Americas by Spanish explorers and settlers. The cowboy tradition in North America can trace its roots back to the vaqueros, who expanded their trade into the southern United States and had an enormous influence even as far north as Canada. Salsa and beans go hand in hand with Mexican cuisine and would have featured heavily in the vaquero diet. These cakes make fantastic veggie burgers.

Can of red kidney beans (19 oz., 540 mL), rinsed and drained	1	1
Large egg	1	1
Crushed tortilla chips	1 cup	250 mL
Medium salsa	1/2 cup	125 mL
Cooking oil	2 tsp.	10 mL

Mash beans with a fork in a medium bowl.

Add next 3 ingredients. Stir well. Divide into 6 equal portions and shape into 3 1/2 inch (9 cm) patties.

Heat cooking oil in a large frying pan on medium. Add patties and cook for about 5 minutes per side, until browned and heated through. Serves 6.

1 serving: 130 Calories; 3.5 g Total Fat (2 g Mono, 0.5 g Poly, 0.5 g Sat); 35 mg Cholesterol; 17 g Carbohydrate (8 g Fibre, 2 g Sugar); 6 g Protein; 350 mg Sodium

Beans were a staple on the trail and would have been included in almost every meal. Chuckwagon cooks had to find creative ways to serve them to keep the cowboys happy. Rather than feeding the men reheated leftover beans, inspired cooks would mash the beans into cakes and pan-fry them, with or without bacon.

Brands

According to Hugh Dempsey's book *The Golden Age of the Canadian Cowboy* (1995), two "rasslers" flipped the calf over, one pulling a hind leg straight out while the other knelt on the neck and held the front legs as the brand was applied to the hind quarter.

A brand is a character or combination of characters burned into the flesh of livestock, primarily cattle and horses. The main purpose of brands is to prove ownership of lost or stolen cattle to deter rustling or to avoid misunderstandings regarding ownership with neighbours. In cowboy-speak, a "maverick" is an unbranded animal of unknown ownership.

When cattle grazed on the open range before waves of settlement took over the West there were two roundups annually, one in the spring, and the other in the autumn. The spring roundup, usually held in June, was often called the "calf" roundup and was for branding the "calf crop" and any newly purchased stock. The cattle were then put out on their summer pastures. The autumn roundup was to gather cattle for shipment to market, and to brand late calves or those missed in the spring.

In the early days, branding irons were heated over open fires. Calves were roped by the hind legs and dragged near the fires to be branded.

Generally, calves were branded on the left side, burning just deep enough into the hide to stop hair from growing out and later covering the brand. The male calves were also de-horned and castrated so they would gain extra weight as steers. It's still a custom at many branding occasions to serve the testicles ("prairie oysters" or "calves' fries") after they've been battered, fried in a skillet and seasoned with salt and pepper.

The practice of branding is still a key event on any ranch and farm in the modern era. Large yearlings are herded into a corral then through a squeeze chute where they are vaccinated and branded. Nowadays a brand is heated by a propane torch, and castration is often administered by stopping the blood flow to the testes using a Burdizzo (a specially designed clamp) or an elastrator band around the testicles to inactivate them, which is considered less intrusive than the old-fashioned way.

Branding has been a legal requirement since 1878 to establish evidence of ownership. In Alberta, for example, all brands must be registered by the Livestock Advisory Committee, established by the Government of Alberta in 1992. After cattle or horse brands are registered, they may be used in one of six positions on an animal:

(1) Cattle: shoulder, rib or hip on either the left or right side.

(2) Horses: jaw, shoulder or thigh on either the left or the right side.

By law, the brand must be applied to the exact part of the animal specified on a brand certificate.

Ranchers take a lot of pride in their brands, which are carried over from one generation to the next, or they may be purchased by new owners. They are a cattleman's trademark, and because hired hands were very loyal to ranch owners, the saying arose that cowboys "rode for the brand."

Trust your neighbour...but brand your cattle.

Butterflied Prairie Oysters

"Prairie oysters" is a polite name for the testicles of bull calves. While they might not appeal to modern urban palates, they've long been a special treat for cowboys and their families following a hard day of branding and neutering bulls in spring. In the cowboy tradition, no part of the cow is wasted, and prairie oysters are customarily breaded and pan-fried, then served before or alongside the main course at supper. Cowboys like to keep things simple but appreciate a little bit of heat in their food, so this recipe stands the test.

Milk	1/2 cup	125 mL
Worcestershire sauce	2 tbsp.	30 mL
Hot sauce	1 tbsp.	15 mL
Large eggs	2	2
Seasoned bread crumbs	3/4 cup	175 mL
Crushed soda crackers	1/4 cup	60 mL
Cayenne pepper	1/2 tsp.	2 mL
Ground nutmeg	1/4 tsp.	1 mL
Calf testicles, cleaned and butterflied	1 lb.	454 g
Cooking oil	3 tbsp.	45 mL

Combine milk, Worcestershire sauce and hot sauce in a large bowl.

In a second bowl, whip eggs so they are foamy.

In a third bowl, combine bread crumbs, soda crackers, cayenne and nutmeg. Dip "oysters" in milk mixture, then in egg and then coat in bread crumb mixture, shaking off excess.

Heat oil in large pan over medium. Fry "oysters" until golden brown. Remove to a plate lined with paper towel to drain. Serve immediately. Serves 4.

1 serving: 400 Calories; 17 g Total Fat (7 g Mono, 3 g Poly, 2 g Sat); 532 mg Cholesterol; 23 g Carbohydrate (trace Fibre, 4 g Sugar); 37 g Protein; 640 mg Sodium

Strip Loin with Blue Cheese

You can't have a cowboy cookbook without a steak recipe, and although this dish doesn't scream traditional cowboy grub, we think all cowboys—urban and rural—will scrape their plates clean. Cheese was an important part of a cowboy's rations back in the day, but it would have been a hard cheese that could keep for months. It was usually added to cooked foods, like soups or bean dishes, rather than eaten on its own.

Brown sugar, packed	1/4 cup	60 mL
Sugar	1/4 cup	60 mL
Seasoning salt	1/4 cup	60 mL
Garlic salt	2 tbsp.	30 mL
Onion salt	1 tbsp.	15 mL
Celery salt	1 1/2 tsp.	7 mL
Paprika	1/4 cup	60 mL
Chili powder	1 tbsp.	15 mL
Pepper	1 tbsp.	15 mL
Allspice	1/2 tsp.	2 mL
Cayenne pepper	1/2 tsp.	2 mL
New York steaks (12 oz., 340 g), room temperature	2	2
Blue cheese	4 oz.	113 g

Preheat barbecue to high. Combine first 11 ingredients in a small bowl. Scoop 1/2 cup (125 mL) mixture into a large plastic bag (reserving remaining rub in airtight container for future use) and add steaks, one at a time, shaking to coat well with rub. Grill steaks for about 7 minutes per side, flipping once. The rub might cause flare-ups, so watch steaks carefully.

Remove steaks from heat and crumble blue cheese over top. Let sit for 5 minutes so cheese warms. Carve steaks into 1 inch (2.5 cm) slices. Serves 4.

1 serving: 410 Calories; 18 g Total Fat (6 g Mono, 1 g Poly, 9 g Sat); 105 mg Cholesterol; 16 g Carbohydrate (2 g Fibre, 12 g Sugar); 46 g Protein; 2680 mg Sodium

A change of pastures makes for a fatter calf.

Easy Pot Roast and Gravy with Mini Yorkshire Puddings

Until relatively recently, a Sunday supper of roast beef was a culinary hallmark on the Canadian prairie. In keeping with English traditions, it was customary to serve the roast beef with Yorkshire puddings and gravy. Serve with peas, roasted carrots and potatoes on the side.

Boneless beef blade (or chuck or round) roast	3 lbs.	1.4 kg
Medium carrot	1	1
Chopped onion	1/2 cup	125 mL
Water	2 cups	500 mL
Garlic powder	1/2 tsp.	2 mL
Ground sage	1/2 tsp.	2 mL
Salt	1/2 tsp.	2 mL
Pepper	1/8 tsp.	0.5 mL
All-purpose flour	2 tbsp.	30 mL
Large eggs, at room temperature	4	4
Milk, at room temperature	1 1/2 cups	375 mL
Melted butter, at room temperature	1/4 cup	60 mL
Prepared horseradish	1 tbsp.	15 mL
Sliced green onion	2 tbsp.	30 mL
Salt	1 tbsp.	15 mL
All-purpose flour	1 1/3 cups	325 mL

Place roast in a small roasting pan. Scatter carrot and onion around roast, and pour water over top.

Sprinkle next 4 ingredients over vegetables. Bake, covered, in 350°F (175°C) oven for 2 to 2 1/2 hours until roast is very tender. Transfer to cutting board. Cover with foil and let sit for 10 minutes before carving.

For the gravy, process drippings, vegetables and first amount of flour in a blender or food processor until smooth, following manufacturer's instructions for processing hot liquids. Transfer to a medium saucepan. Cook, stirring, on medium until boiling and thickened.

For the puddings, heat a muffin tin in a 450°F (230°C) oven. Mix eggs, milk and butter together extremely well.

(continued on next page)

Combine horseradish, green onion, salt and second amount of flour in a small bowl. Add to milk mixture, scraping sides of bowl to incorporate all of flour. Remove empty muffin tin from oven and spray with cooking spray, then fill 8 cups to about half full. Bake for 25 minutes. DO NOT OPEN OVEN EARLY. Place puddings on a wire rack to cool. Serves 8.

1 serving: 560 Calories; 34 g Total Fat (14 g Mono, 1.5 g Poly, 14 g Sat); 230 mg Cholesterol; 22 g Carbohydrate (1 g Fibre, 4 g Sugar); 37 g Protein; 1230 mg Sodium

Peppered Beef Dip

*The secret to this tasty recipe is to slow cook the roast to tenderize it.
A chuckwagon cook would have used his trusty Dutch oven to cook the
meat, but a slow cooker works just as well. Beef broth and onion soup keep
the roast moist and impart a unique flavour to the au jus. Try adding some
thinly sliced red Spanish onion marinated in red wine vinegar to the beef in
a bun for an even greater tangy taste.*

Boneless beef blade (or chuck) roast	3 lbs.	1.4 kg
Pepper	1 tbsp.	15 mL
Can of condensed beef broth (10 oz., 284 mL)	1	1
Can of condensed onion soup (10 oz., 284 mL)	1	1
Panini buns, split	6	6

Sprinkle roast with pepper. Heat a large greased frying pan on medium-high. Add roast. Cook for about 8 minutes, turning occasionally, until browned on all sides. Transfer to a 4 to 5 quart (4 to 5 L) slow cooker or Dutch oven.

Add broth and soup to same frying pan. Cook, stirring and scraping any brown bits from bottom of pan, until boiling. Pour over roast. Cook, covered, on Low for 8 to 9 hours or on High for 4 to 4 1/2 hours for a slow cooker or for about 2 hours in a 325°F (160°C) oven for a Dutch oven. Transfer roast to cutting board. Cover with foil. Let stand for 10 minutes. Skim and discard fat from cooking liquid. Carefully process in blender, following manufacturer's directions for processing hot liquids, until smooth. Cut roast into thin slices.

Fill buns with beef. Cut each bun in half. Serve with small bowl of cooking liquid for dipping. Serves 12.

1 serving: *360 Calories; 21 g Total Fat (9 g Mono, 1 g Poly, 8 g Sat); 80 mg Cholesterol; 17 g Carbohydrate (2 g Fibre, 2 g Sugar); 25 g Protein; 650 mg Sodium*

To cook this dish outdoors in a cast iron or aluminum Dutch oven, place 9 briquettes under its base and 11 on the lid.

Beefsteak with Gravy

A steak that is served as a cutlet would be a real treat for cowboys on the trail or range, who traditionally cooked over a campfire and ate slightly charred meat. Beefsteak, also known as chicken fried steak, was popular among cowboys in the American southwest and found its way onto the plates of cowboys in Canada thanks to the rather fluid border between Canada and the U.S. during the days of the great cattle drives. The addition of garlic, onion salt, pepper, paprika and chili really adds to the appeal of this dish.

Half-and-half cream	1 1/2 cups	375 mL
Large eggs	2	2
Bread crumbs	2 cups	500 mL
Garlic salt	1 tsp.	5 mL
Onion salt	1 tsp.	5 mL
Paprika	3/4 tsp.	4 mL
Chili powder	1/2 tsp.	2 mL
Pepper	1/2 tsp.	2 mL
Sirloin steak, well tenderized	3 lbs.	1.4 kg
Cooking oil	1/2 cup	125 mL
All-purpose flour	1/3 cup	75 mL
Milk	3 1/2 cups	875 mL
Seasoning salt	1/2 tsp.	2 mL
Pepper	1/2 tsp.	2 mL

Whisk together cream and eggs in a large bowl. Combine bread crumbs, garlic salt, onion salt, paprika, chili powder and first amount of pepper in a separate bowl.

Cut steak into 6 equal pieces. Dip each piece into egg mixture and then into bread crumb mixture, shaking off excess coating. Place onto a clean plate.

Heat oil in a large pan over medium. Add steaks and cook until edges start to look golden brown, about 2 minutes each side, working in batches, if necessary. Remove meat to a plate lined with paper towel, cover with foil and set aside.

For the gravy, drain all but 1/4 cup (60 mL) oil from pan and reheat to medium. Sprinkle flour evenly over oil and whisk, creating a roux. Cook roux for about 3 minutes, constantly whisking.

(continued on next page)

Pour in milk and whisk constantly. Add seasoning salt and second amount of pepper and whisk until you have a smooth, thick gravy, about 7 minutes. Add more milk if gravy becomes too thick. Serve steak with gravy poured over top. Serves 6.

1 serving: 910 Calories; 54 g Total Fat (23 g Mono, 3.5 g Poly, 22 g Sat); 265 mg Cholesterol; 47 g Carbohydrate (2 g Fibre, 9 g Sugar); 62 g Protein; 1440 mg Sodium

Don't squat with your spurs on.

Cowboy Music

Ninety percent of cowboy songs in Canada and the United States came from Scotland and Ireland, because many of the cowboys hailed from there in the early days. For example, "The Streets of Laredo" began as a folk song known as "The Unfortunate Rake" in 18th-century Ireland. It has become one of the top cowboy songs of all time. One of our co-authors went to Scotland some years ago and in a bar encountered people who sang the song in Gaelic.

The first verse is as follows:

> As I walked out in the streets of Laredo
> As I walked out in Laredo one day,
> I spied a poor cowboy all wrapped in white linen
> All wrapped in white linen and cold as the clay.

The song goes on to tell the sad story of the cowboy, who knew he'd done wrong, being shot in the chest. The haunting music has been recorded countless times by countless artists, has travelled through the generations and can still be heard today.

Another popular early cowboy song is "Git Along, Little Dogies," which has also been recorded many times. A dogie is a stray calf, motherless usually, whose belly swelled up because it was weaned too early and had to survive by eating indigestible rough grass. The cowboys called the calves "dough-guts," which over time evolved into "dogies."

On a cattle drive, the night shift was by far the hardest for cowboys. In the dark, any small thing could spook the cattle and start a stampede. To keep the cows calm, cowboys would circle the herd on horseback, singing to them.

Buckaroo Burgers

"Buckaroo" is slang for cowboy, and a burger just doesn't get any more cowboy than this one, which is loaded with bacon and cheese and topped with seasoned onion rings.

Lean ground beef	1 lb.	454 g
Large egg, fork beaten	1	1
Seasoned bread crumbs	1/4 cup	60 mL
Grated Cheddar cheese	1/2 cup	125 mL
Garlic cloves, minced	2	2
Cooking oil	2 tbsp.	30 mL
All-purpose flour	1/4 cup	60 mL
Paprika	1 tsp.	5 mL
Ground thyme	1/2 tsp.	2 mL
Salt	1/4 tsp.	1 mL
Thinly sliced onions	1/2 cup	125 mL
Large egg, fork beaten	1	1
Cooking oil	1/4 cup	60 mL
Hamburger buns, toasted	4	4
Barbecue sauce	4 tbsp.	60 mL
Mustard	4 tbsp.	60 mL
Cheese slices (optional)	4	4
Pickle slices	8	8
Cooked bacon slices	8	8
Leaves green leaf lettuce	4	4

Combine ground beef, first egg, bread crumbs and grated cheese in a large bowl. Shape into 4 patties, about 5 inches (12.5 cm) in diameter. Heat first amount of oil in a large frying pan over medium. Cook patties for about 6 minutes per side until no longer pink inside.

Combine flour, paprika, thyme and salt in a medium bowl. Dip onion slices into second egg and then coat in flour mixture.

Heat second amount of oil in a small pan over medium. Carefully place battered pieces of onion into hot oil and fry for about 3 minutes until brown and crispy, working in batches if necessary. Drain on a paper towel.

Open hamburger buns and spread 1 tbsp. (15 mL) barbecue sauce and 1 tbsp. (15 mL) mustard on bottom of each bun. Top with patty, cheese slice (if using), pickles, bacon, fried onions and lettuce. Cover with top half of each bun. Serves 4.

1 serving: 1100 Calories; 75 g Total Fat (31 g Mono, 8 g Poly, 27 g Sat); 260 mg Cholesterol; 45 g Carbohydrate (2 g Fibre, 4 g Sugar); 49 g Protein, 1810 mg Sodium

Don't worry about biting off more than you can chew; your mouth is probably a whole lot bigger than you think.

Sloppy Joes

Sloppy Joes apparently originated in a café in Sioux City, Iowa, in 1930 and have since become popular throughout North America. They are an American "sandwich" convention, so to speak, with a filling of browned ground meat that has been seasoned with a sauce of tomatoes and various spices. Today they are usually served in hamburger buns or kaisers, but historically cowboys would have used biscuits.

Cooking oil	2 tsp.	10 mL
Lean ground beef	2 lbs.	900 g
Can of tomato sauce (14 oz., 398 mL)	1	1
Chopped onion	1 1/2 cups	375 mL
Thinly sliced celery	1 cup	250 mL
Barbecue sauce	2 tbsp.	30 mL
Worcestershire sauce	2 tsp.	10 mL
Salt, to taste		
Pepper, to taste		
Grated medium Cheddar cheese	1 1/2 cups	375 mL
Kaiser rolls, split (toasted, optional)	8	8

Heat cooking oil in a large frying pan on medium. Add ground beef and scramble-fry for 5 to 10 minutes until no longer pink. Drain and transfer to a slow cooker or Dutch oven.

Stir in next 7 ingredients. Cook, covered, on Low for 8 to 9 hours or on High for 4 to 4 1/2 hours for a slow cooker or in a 350°F (160°C) oven for 2 hours for a Dutch oven.

Add cheese and stir until melted.

Spoon beef mixture onto bottom half of each roll and cover with top half. Serves 8.

1 serving: 560 Calories; 25 g Total Fat (10 g Mono, 1 g Poly, 11 g Sat); 90 mg Cholesterol; 39 g Carbohydrate (4 g Fibre, 6 g Sugar); 36 g Protein; 950 mg Sodium

A burr in your own saddle is a pain; a burr is someone else's saddle is entertainment.

Whisky Dijon Meatballs

Where would a cowboy be without whisky, which is as much a part of cowboy culture as rum is to sailors? Blended with some spicy Dijon mustard, whisky brings out the best in meatballs, long considered a comfort food and always a treat on farms and ranches, no matter the season. Cowboy meatballs are customarily on the large size, a testament to the cowboys' hearty appetites.

Ground beef	2 lbs.	900 g
Seasoned bread crumbs	1 cup	250 mL
Large egg	1	1
Grated onion	2/3 cup	150 mL
Garlic cloves, minced	2	2
Montreal steak spice	2 tsp.	10 mL
Pepper	1/4 tsp.	1 mL
Grainy Dijon mustard	2 tsp.	10 mL
Cooking oil	2 tbsp.	30 mL
Whisky	1 cup	250 mL
Beef broth	3 cups	750 mL
Grainy Dijon mustard	3 tbsp.	45 mL
Worcestershire sauce	3 tbsp.	45 mL
Half and half cream	1 cup	250 mL
Salt	1/4 tsp.	1 mL
Pepper	1/4 tsp.	1 mL

In a large bowl combine beef, bread crumbs, egg, onion, garlic, steak spice and first amounts of pepper and mustard. Mix well. Shape into meatballs, using 2 tbsp. (30 mL) mixture per meatball. Place each meatball on a lined baking sheet.

Heat 1 tbsp. (15 mL) cooking oil in a large frying pan over medium-high. Working in batches, cook meatballs for 6 to 8 minutes until cooked through, adding more cooking oil as needed. Remove cooked meatballs from pan and drain on a plate lined with paper towel. Set aside.

For the sauce, combine whisky and broth in a large saucepan. Bring to a simmer and cook for about 3 minutes.

Stir in second amount of mustard and Worcestershire sauce. Add cream, salt and second amount of pepper and bring to a low simmer. Cook sauce for an additional 3 minutes, never allowing it to boil. Add meatballs to sauce and cook for another 3 minutes or until heated through. Remove from heat and serve immediately. Serves 8.

1 serving: 460 Calories; 20 g Total Fat (8 g Mono, 0.5 g Poly, 9 g Sat); 105 mg Cholesterol; 18 g Carbohydrate (trace Fibre, 3 g Sugar); 27 g Protein; 1000 mg Sodium

Shepherd's Pie

Shepherd's pie, by definition, is a baked dish of ground or diced meat topped with various chopped vegetables beneath a layer of mashed potatoes. It has long been a go-to recipe across North America because all the work is done up front, perfect comfort food after a long day's work. It's especially popular as an evening meal during the long, cold winter months. What stands out in this recipe is that the horseradish and paprika give the shepherd's pie a pleasant amount of added heat.

Medium potatoes, peeled and cut up	4	4
Milk	3 tbsp.	45 mL
Butter (or hard margarine)	1 tbsp.	15 mL
Seasoned salt	1/2 tsp.	2 mL
Cooking oil	2 tsp.	10 mL
Lean ground beef	1 1/2 lbs	680 g
Chopped onion	1 cup	250 mL
All-purpose flour	1 tbsp.	15 mL
Salt	1 1/2 tsp.	7 mL
Pepper	1/4 tsp.	1 mL
Milk	1/3 cup	75 mL
Cooked peas	1 cup	250 mL
Cooked sliced carrot	1 cup	250 mL
Ketchup	1 tbsp.	15 mL
Worcestershire sauce	1 tsp.	5 mL
Prepared horseradish	1 tsp.	5 mL
Butter (or hard margarine), melted	2 tbsp.	30 mL
Paprika, sprinkle		

Cook potato in boiling salted water in a large saucepan until tender. Drain.

Add first amount of milk, butter and seasoned salt to saucepan and mash. Cover and set aside.

Heat cooking oil in a large frying pan on medium. Add beef and onion. Scramble-fry for about 10 minutes until beef is no longer pink. Drain.

Stir in next 3 ingredients. Slowly add second amount of milk, stirring constantly. Cook, stirring, for about 2 minutes until boiling and thickened.

(continued on next page)

Stir in next 5 ingredients. Spread in greased 2 quart (2 L) shallow baking dish. Spread mashed potatoes on beef mixture.

Brush with melted butter. Sprinkle with paprika. Bake, uncovered, in 350°F (175°C) oven for about 30 minutes until heated through and potatoes are golden. Serves 6.

1 serving: 410 Calories; 18 g Total Fat (7 g Mono, 1 g Poly, 8 g Sat); 60 mg Cholesterol; 36 g Carbohydrate (4 g Fibre, 7 g Sugar); 20 g Protein; 910 mg Sodium

Hamburger Hash

Cowboys are not known for being fussy eaters, so hash wouldn't offend their sensibilities. Hamburger hash is a dish of ground beef that is pan-fried with basically whatever ingredients are on hand, though potatoes are a standard ingredient. It doesn't take a lot of culinary skill to make hash, and it would have given a chuckwagon cook a tasty way to use up random ingredients before they passed their prime. We've used frozen mixed veggies in this recipe, but feel free to use whatever fresh or frozen veggies you have on hand.

Cooking oil	2 tsp.	10 mL
Lean ground beef	1 lb.	454 g
Chopped onion	1 cup	250 mL
Chopped celery	1/4 cup	60 mL
All-purpose flour	2 tbsp.	30 mL
Beef bouillon powder	1 tbsp.	15 mL
Celery salt	1/2 tsp.	2 mL
Onion powder	1/2 tsp.	2 mL
Water	1 1/4 cups	300 mL
Frozen hash brown potatoes	2 cups	500 mL
Frozen mixed vegetables	1 1/2 cups	375 mL

Heat cooking oil in a large frying pan on medium. Add ground beef, onion and celery. Scramble-fry for about 10 minutes until beef is no longer pink. Drain.

Stir in next 4 ingredients. Add water. Cook, stirring, for about 1 minute until boiling and thickened.

Add potatoes and vegetables. Cook for about 10 minutes, stirring occasionally, until heated through. Serves 4.

1 serving: 520 Calories; 27 g Total Fat (12 g Mono, 8 g Poly, 10 g Sat); 70 mg Cholesterol; 35 g Carbohydrate (3 g Fibre, 5 g Sugar); 27 g Protein; 990 mg Sodium

When in doubt, let your horse do the thinking.

Cowboy Casserole

Farm and ranch cooks are big fans of all things casserole because they can never be certain when cowboys will finish a day's work. This casserole stands out from its peers because of the mixture of cream of mushroom and cream of chicken soup as well as the addition of potato tots. Comfort food at its finest, this casserole is a meal in itself, or it could be paired with a tossed salad with ranch dressing and croutons.

Cooking oil	1 tsp.	5 mL
Lean ground beef	2 lbs.	900 g
Chopped onion	1 cup	250 mL
Can of condensed cream of mushroom soup (10 oz., 284 mL)	1	1
Can of condensed cream of chicken soup (10 oz., 284 mL)	1	1
Milk	1 cup	250 mL
Salt	1 tsp.	5 mL
Pepper	1/4 tsp.	1 mL
Package of frozen potato tots (2 1/4 lbs., 1 kg)	1	1
Grated light sharp Cheddar cheese	1 cup	250 mL

Heat cooking oil in a large frying pan on medium. Add beef and onion. Scramble-fry for about 10 minutes until beef is no longer pink. Drain.

Stir in next 5 ingredients. Spread in greased 9 x 13 inch (23 x 33 cm) pan.

Arrange potato tots on beef mixture. Bake, uncovered, in 350°F (175°C) oven for 1 hour.

Sprinkle with cheese. Bake for another 10 to 15 minutes until cheese is melted. Serves 8.

1 serving: 650 Calories; 36 g Total Fat (13 g Mono, 2.5 g Poly, 15 g Sat); 80 mg Cholesterol; 44 g Carbohydrate (4 g Fibre, 3 g Sugar); 32 g Protein; 1820 mg Sodium

Mac 'n' Cheese 'n' Meat

This hearty meal would often be served after a day of baling hay under the hot August sun or following a day building barbed wire fences. Always a family favourite, the sharp taste of Cheddar cheese is what makes this recipe stand out as a go-to comfort food. Try it with a bottle of chilled French chardonnay wine.

Cooking oil	2 tsp.	10 mL
Ground beef	1 lb.	454 g
Elbow macaroni	2 cups	500 mL
Butter (or hard margarine)	1/4 cup	60 mL
All-purpose flour	3 tbsp.	45 mL
Onion flakes	1 tbsp.	15 mL
Salt	1/2 tsp.	2 mL
Pepper	1/8 tsp.	0.5 mL
Milk	2 cups	500 mL
Grated medium (or sharp) Cheddar cheese	1 cup	250 mL
Butter (or hard margarine)	2 tbsp.	30 mL
Fine dry bread crumbs	1/2 cup	125 mL
Grated medium (or sharp) Cheddar cheese	1/4 cup	60 mL

Heat cooking oil in a large frying pan on medium. Add beef and scramble-fry for about 10 minutes, until no longer pink. Drain and transfer to a greased 3 quart (3 L) casserole.

Cook macaroni in boiling salted water in a large uncovered saucepan or Dutch oven for 8 to 10 minutes, stirring occasionally, until tender but firm. Drain. Add to beef and stir.

Melt first amount of butter in same saucepan on medium. Add next 4 ingredients. Cook, stirring, for 1 minute.

Slowly add milk, stirring constantly until smooth. Cook, stirring, for about 5 minutes until boiling and thickened. Remove from heat. Add first amount of cheese. Stir until melted. Add to macaroni mixture and stir.

Melt second amount of butter in a small saucepan. Remove from heat. Add bread crumbs and second amount of cheese. Stir until well mixed. Sprinkle over macaroni mixture. Bake, uncovered, in 350°F (175°C) oven for about 30 minutes until golden. Serves 4.

1 serving: 920 Calories; 51 g Total Fat (16 g Mono, 2.5 g Poly, 27 g Sat); 165 mg Cholesterol; 61 g Carbohydrate (2 g Fibre, 9 g Sugar); 45 g Protein; 880 mg Sodium

Smoky Grilled Beef Jerky

True, jerky is not actually a main, but many a cowboy would have a stash of jerky in his saddle bags for days on the trail. In fact, jerky and a few leftover biscuits might be all a cowboy would eat from morning until nightfall, when he would head back to the chuckwagon for a warm meal. This eclectic recipe combines the bourbon, Louisiana hot sauce and hickory flavours of the Cajun south with the Oriental flavour of soy sauce in a flank steak, which always takes well to marinades. Serve with some potato chips and wash the beef jerky down with a cool lager or pale ale.

Soy sauce	1/3 cup	75 mL
Bourbon whiskey	1/4 cup	60 mL
Brown sugar, packed	1/4 cup	60 mL
White vinegar	1/4 cup	60 mL
Worcestershire sauce	2 tbsp.	30 mL
Chili powder	1 tbsp.	15 mL
Garlic powder	1 tbsp.	15 mL
Louisiana hot sauce	2 tsp.	10 mL
Pepper	2 tsp.	10 mL
Flank steak, trimmed of fat, thinly sliced across the grain (1/8 inch, 3 mm, slices)	1 lb.	454 g
Hickory wood chips, soaked in water for 4 hours and drained	2 cups	500 mL

Combine first 9 ingredients in a medium bowl.

Put beef into a large resealable freezer bag. Pour soy sauce mixture over top. Seal bag and turn until beef is coated. Marinate in refrigerator for at least 6 hours or overnight, turning occasionally. Remove beef. Discard any remaining soy sauce mixture.

Put wood chips into a smoker box. Place smoker box on 1 burner. Turn on burner under smoker box to high. When smoke appears, adjust burner to maintain interior barbecue temperature of medium-low. Arrange beef evenly on a sheet of heavy-duty (or double layer of regular) foil. Place on an ungreased grill over unlit burner. Close lid. Cook for about 1 hour until darkened. Blot dry with paper towel. Turn beef. Rotate foil 180°. Close lid. Cook for about 2 hours, rotating foil 180° at halftime, until beef is dried but still flexible. Cool completely. Makes about 35 pieces.

1 piece: 35 Calories; 1 g Total Fat (0 g Mono, 0 g Poly, 0 g Sat); 5 mg Cholesterol; 2 g Carbohydrate (0 g Fibre, 2 g Sugar); 3 g Protein; 160 mg Sodium

Chuckwagons

Texas rancher and cattle drive pioneer Charles (Charlie) Goodnight is credited with inventing the chuckwagon (also known as a "mess wagon") in 1866. He and Oliver Loving drove their first herd of longhorn cattle northward from Texas to New Mexico along what would become known as the Goodnight-Loving Trail. Goodnight adapted an army surplus wagon to serve as a mobile kitchen on that long-distance cattle drive. Before long, chuckwagons became a fixture associated with virtually all cattle drives, as well as all significant roundups.

The dinner bell is always in tune.

It was the cook's job to get the chuckwagon ready for a cattle drive or roundup. He'd scrub the cupboards with boiling water and lye soap to clean them. Pots, pans and eating utensils were scoured with soap and sand. The water barrel was cleaned and soaked to make sure the seams swelled so it wouldn't leak. Wagon axles were greased, the harness mended and horses or oxen broken in.

The cook was a key member of the crew, in charge of the food. In the cattle drive and roundup pecking order, a cook generally outranked all other members except the trail boss, and he was a person to be treated with respect by all cowboys. Most camp cooks also had a working knowledge of practical medicine and were in charge of medical supplies. The cook travelled ahead of the cattle drive and had meals prepared when the crew stopped for the night. Just about all camp cooks had a reputation for being cantankerous—understandable considering the long hours they worked.

The chuckwagon contained all the necessities for cooking: an iron stove, cook tent, tin plates and utensils. A mess box was bolted on the back of the wagon, fitted with a hinged door and a leg brace so that when it was lowered, it became a table for the cook. The mess box was called a "chuck-box." The stove was attached to one side of the wagon, a water barrel on the other side. An iron triangle hanging on the wagon would be clanged to summon the cowboys when meals were ready. Salt, sugar, tea and coffee were stored in pails with tight-fitting lids in the chuckwagon. Sacks of flour and beans, cases of dried fruits and canned milk and tomatoes were stored in the bed of the wagon. Firewood was usually carried in a separate wagon that also was used to transport all the cowboys' bedrolls and other necessary gear.

Country-style Pork Ribs

Beef may have reigned supreme among cowboys, put pork also had its place on the menu. On the trail, cured pork—especially bacon—was the norm, but most of the larger ranches raised at least a few pigs, so fresh pork was sometimes available. The secret to the best tasting ribs is to cook them slowly at a low heat so they don't dry out. For a real southern feel, use the mesquite barbecue sauce and wood chips in this dish.

Barbecue sauce (mesquite or hickory flavour is best)	1 cup	250 mL
Liquid honey	1/4 cup	60 mL
Soy sauce	1 tbsp.	15 mL
Chopped onion	1/2 cup	125 mL
Garlic cloves, minced (or 1/2 tsp., 2 mL, powder), optional	2	2
Country-style pork rib ends, trimmed	3 lbs.	1.4 kg
Mesquite (or hickory) wood chips	1 1/2 cups	375 mL

Combine first 5 ingredients in a small bowl. Pour into a shallow dish or resealable freezer bag. Add ribs. Turn to coat. Marinate, covered or sealed, in refrigerator for at least 4 hours or up to 24 hours, turning several times.

Put 3/4 cup (175 mL) dry wood chips into a smoker box. Soak remaining 3/4 cup (175 mL) chips in water in a medium bowl for 15 to 30 minutes. Drain. Place on top of dry chips. Close smoker box and place on grill on 1 side of gas barbecue. Close lid. Heat barbecue to medium for 15 to 20 minutes until chips are smoking. Adjust burner under smoker box as necessary to keep it smoking. Adjust opposite burner to maintain medium-low barbecue temperature. Remove grill opposite smoker box using oven mitts. Place a drip pan, with 1 inch (2.5 cm) water, directly on heat source. Replace grill. Drain and discard marinade. Arrange ribs on greased grill over drip pan and close lid. Cook for 1 hour. Turn ribs. Replenish water in pan if necessary. Cook ribs for 15 to 20 minutes until tender and glazed. Serves 6.

1 serving: 460 Calories; 19 g Total Fat (8 g Mono, 2 g Poly, 6 g Sat); 160 mg Cholesterol; 36 g Carbohydrate (0 g Fibre, 11 g Sugar); 46 g Protein; 880 mg Sodium

Sweet Smoky Ribs

Every cook's dream is for "falling apart" ribs, and this slow cooker recipe will make such a dream come true. When done, the ribs should be permeated with the flavour of molasses and soy sauce, plus they'll have a wee bit of heat from the crushed chilies and a bit of a bite from the garlic, with the meat almost literally falling of the bones! For an authentic cowboy meal, enjoy these ribs with a side dish of baked beans or coleslaw.

Fancy (mild) molasses	1/3 cup	75 mL
Low-sodium soy sauce	1/3 cup	75 mL
Garlic cloves, minced	3	3
Dried crushed chilies	1/4 tsp.	1 mL
Sweet and sour cut pork ribs, trimmed of fat and cut into 1-bone portions	3 1/2 lbs.	1.6 kg

Combine first 4 ingredients in a slow cooker or Dutch oven.

Add ribs. Stir until coated. Cook, stirring occasionally, on Low for 7 to 8 hours or on High for 3 1/2 to 4 hours for a slow cooker, or in a 325°F (160°C) oven for about 2 hours for a Dutch oven. Serves 6.

1 serving: 680 Calories; 46 g Total Fat (20 g Mono, 4 g Poly, 17 g Sat); 175 mg Cholesterol; 16 g Carbohydrate (0 g Fibre, 12 g Sugar); 48 g Protein; 750 mg Sodium

Cranberry Apple Pork Roast

Pork would be a welcome change in the diet of cowboys, who tend to be beef eaters. Back in the day, almost every farm and ranch would have had a pig pen where swine would be raised for cash sales and personal use. Swine are the original recyclers, so farm and ranch wives would always save what they called "slop" (i.e., waste food and table scraps) for the pig trough.

Boneless pork roast	4 lbs.	1.8 kg
Salt	1/4 tsp.	1 mL
Pepper	1/4 tsp.	1 mL
Frozen (or fresh) cranberries	3 cups	750 mL
Chopped peeled cooking apple (such as McIntosh)	2 cups	500 mL
Liquid honey	1/2 cup	125 mL
Frozen concentrated apple juice	3 tbsp.	45 mL

Place roast in a large roasting pan and sprinkle with salt and pepper. Cook, uncovered, in 400°F (200°C) oven for 30 minutes. Reduce heat to 325°F (160°C). Cook, uncovered, for about 45 minutes until meat thermometer inserted into thickest part of roast reads at least 155°F (68°C) or more depending on desired doneness. Transfer to cutting board. Tent with foil. Let stand for 10 minutes. Cut roast into thin slices. Arrange on serving platter.

For the sauce, combine remaining 4 ingredients in a medium saucepan and bring to a boil. Reduce heat to medium and simmer, uncovered, for about 10 minutes, stirring occasionally, until cranberries are soft. Spoon over pork and serve. Serves 12.

1 serving: 350 Calories; 9 g Total Fat (4 g Mono, 1 g Poly, 3 g Sat); 95 mg Cholesterol; 27 g Carbohydrate (2 g Fibre, 22 g Sugar); 37 g Protein; 130 mg Sodium

Quesadillas on the Grill ✓

This recipe is another dish that pays tribute to the cowboys' vaquero roots. Tortillas filled with tender grilled chicken breasts lightly marinated with lime juice are cooked to perfection over a campfire or on a pre-heated grill and topped with the classic Tex-Mex flavours of avocado, tomato and sour cream.

Boneless, skinless chicken breasts	4	4
Squeeze of fresh lime juice		
Large flour tortillas	4	4
Salsa	1 3/4 cups	425 mL
Grated Cheddar or mozzarella cheese, or a combination	2 cups	500 mL
Chopped shallots	2 tbsp.	30 mL
Guacamole, sour cream and diced tomato for serving		

Preheat grill to medium. Cook chicken until meat is no longer pink and juices run clear. Squeeze a bit of lime juice over chicken and set aside.

Take each tortilla and spread salsa, cheese and shallots on half of each one.

Slice chicken into 1/2 inch (12 mm) thick strips and place on tortillas, with strips radiating from middle toward edge. Fold each tortilla in half and place on grill on low—avoid high flames or high heat. Cook for 2 minutes. Flip tortillas and cook for another 2 minutes.

Remove tortillas from grill and cut into pie-shaped wedges with a pizza cutter. Serve with guacamole, sour cream and tomato. Serves 4.

1 serving: 780 Calories; 27 g Total Fat (9 g Mono, 2 g Poly, 14 g Sat); 195 mg Cholesterol; 54 g Carbohydrate (6 g Fibre, 8 g Sugar); 77 g Protein; 1760 mg Sodium

Barbecued Chicken √

*After beef, chicken would be high on the list of cowboys' favourite meals.
It wasn't often available to cowboys on the trail, but most ranches would have
had a chicken coop. Back in the day, whole chickens would most likely have
been roasted over an open fire, but we've opted to butterfly the chicken and
cook it with indirect heat on the barbecue instead. Lemon pepper is particularly
tasty as a seasoning for poultry.*

Butter (or hard margarine), softened	3 tbsp.	45 mL
Worcestershire sauce	1 tbsp.	15 mL
Liquid honey	1 tbsp.	15 mL
Lemon pepper	2 tsp.	10 mL
Dried oregano	3/4 tsp.	4 mL
Garlic cloves, minced (or 1/2 tsp., 2 mL, powder)	2	2
Whole roasting chicken	3 1/2 lbs.	1.6 kg

Combine first 6 ingredients in a small bowl.

Place chicken, breast side down, on a cutting board. Using kitchen shears
or a sharp knife, cut down both sides of backbone to remove. Turn chicken,
breast side up. Press chicken out flat. Carefully loosen, but do not remove,
skin. Stuff butter mixture between flesh and skin, spreading mixture as
evenly as possible. Preheat gas barbecue to medium. Turn off centre or left
burner. Place chicken, stuffed side down, on greased grill over drip pan on
unlit side. Close lid. Cook for 35 minutes. Carefully turn chicken and cook
for 55 to 60 minutes, until meat thermometer inserted in thigh reads 180°F
(82°C). Let stand for 15 minutes. Cut into serving-size pieces. Serves 5.

*1 serving: 780 Calories; 68 g Total Fat (2 g Mono, 0 g Poly, 4.5 g Sat); 215 mg Cholesterol;
5 g Carbohydrate (0 g Fibre, 4 g Sugar); 37 g Protein; 220 mg Sodium*

Pizza on the Grill

Pizza is obviously not traditional cowboy fare, but with their affinity for biscuits, cowboys of old would have loved this recipe! This modern-day cowboy treat goes down well with a cold beer. It's not hard to make your own pizza, and you can incorporate any ingredients that suit your tastes once you get the hang of it. For pizza-making newbies, however, just follow the simple steps in this recipe and you won't go wrong. You'll be using the convection heat in your barbecue, not unlike chefs who use a commercial kitchen pizza oven.

Biscuit mix	2 cups	500 mL
Milk	1/2 cup	125 mL
Pasta (or pizza) sauce	1 cup	250 mL
Grated part-skim mozzarella cheese	2 cups	500 mL
Sliced fresh white mushrooms	1 cup	250 mL
Chopped deli meat	1 cup	250 mL
Chopped green onion	1/2 cup	125 mL
Chopped red pepper	1/2 cup	125 mL
Grated part-skim mozzarella cheese	1 cup	250 mL

Measure biscuit mix into a medium bowl and add milk. Stir until just moistened. Turn out dough onto lightly floured surface. Knead 8 to 10 times. Press evenly in greased 12 inch (30 cm) pizza pan. Preheat barbecue to high. Place pan on 1 side of ungreased grill. Turn off burner under pan, turning opposite burner down to medium. Close lid. Cook for about 15 minutes, rotating pan at halftime, until crust is just starting to turn golden.

Spread pasta sauce evenly over crust. Sprinkle first amount of mozzarella cheese over sauce and layer next 4 ingredients, in order given, over cheese. Sprinkle with second amount of cheese. Return to unlit side of grill. Close lid. Cook for about 15 minutes until heated through and cheese is melted. Cut into 6 wedges. Serves 6.

1 serving: 450 Calories; 18 g Total Fat (1 g Mono, 0 g Poly, 8 g Sat); 45 mg Cholesterol; 48 g Carbohydrate (3 g Fibre, 7 g Sugar); 20 g Protein; 1770 mg Sodium

Crispy Pan-fried Chicken

On the trail cowboys ate mostly beef, so delicious pan-fried chicken would be a welcome change once they returned to the ranch. Serve this dish with coleslaw or a potato salad and a glass of cool lemonade.

All-purpose flour	3/4 cup	175 mL
Paprika	1 tsp.	5 mL
Ground thyme	1 tsp.	5 mL
Salt	1 tsp.	5 mL
Pepper	1/4 tsp.	1 mL
Large egg	1	1
Milk	2 tbsp.	30 mL
Lemon juice	2 tsp.	10 mL
Bone-in chicken parts	3 lbs.	1.4 kg
Cooking oil	1/4 cup	60 mL

Combine first 5 ingredients in a shallow dish.

Beat egg in a separate shallow dish. Stir in milk and lemon juice.

Dip chicken into flour mixture, then into egg mixture. Dip back into flour mixture until coated. Let stand for 30 minutes.

Heat cooking oil in a cast iron frying pan to medium high. Working in batches, fry chicken for 10 to 12 minutes, turning twice, until cooked through. Remove to plate lined with paper towel to drain. Serve immediately. Serves 5.

1 serving: 940 Calories; 77 g Total Fat (13 g Mono, 0.5 g Poly, 16 g Sat); 280 mg Cholesterol; 15 g Carbohydrate (trace Fibre, trace Sugar); 44 g Protein; 550 mg Sodium

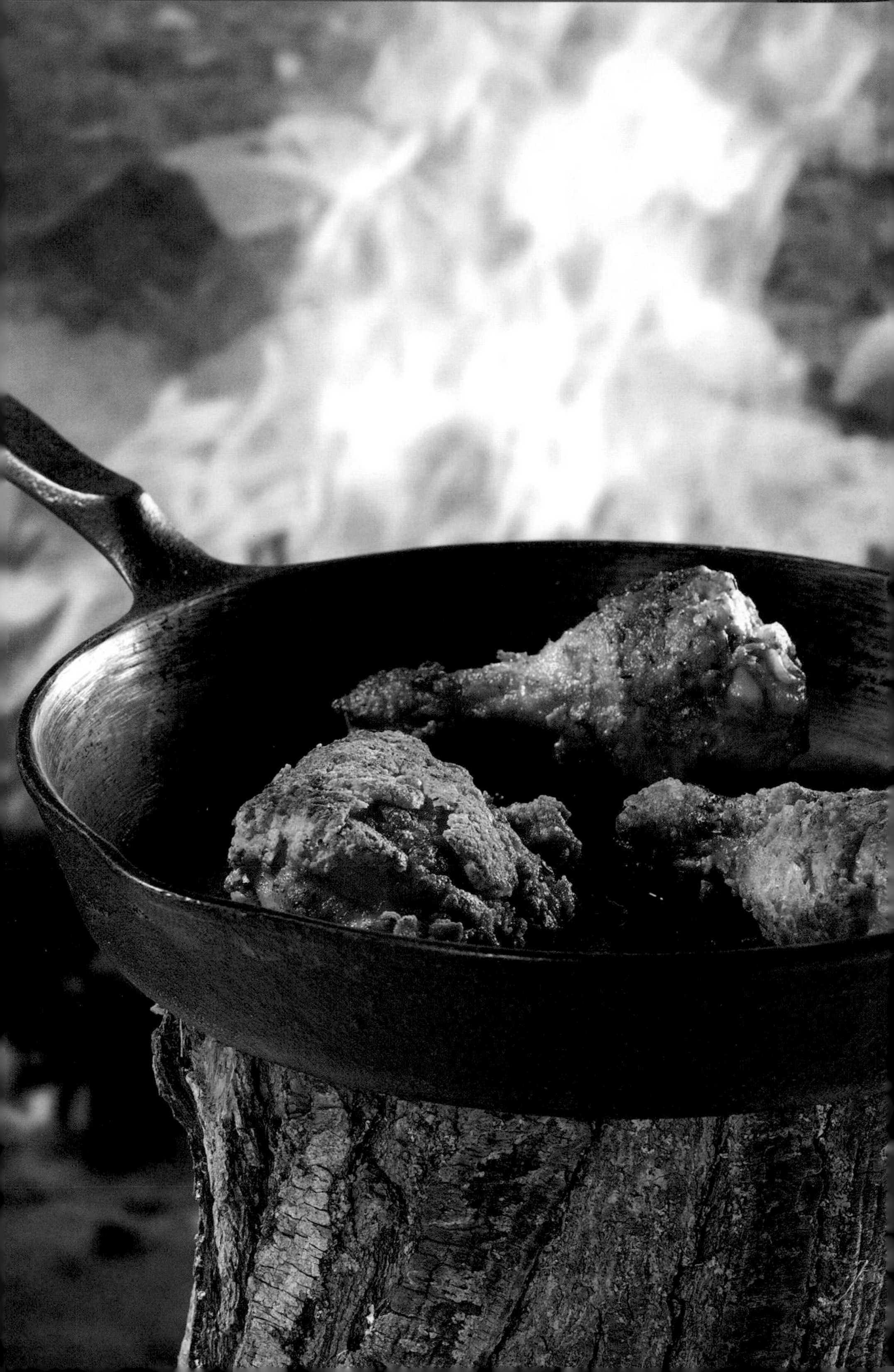

Dutch Ovens

While there could occasionally be some lean times on cattle drives, they would be the exception because well-managed outfits always provided plenty of staple food. There was a saying on cattle drives and roundups, "We don't set out to starve none."

A Dutch oven is a thick-sided cooking pot constructed in various shapes and sizes, usually made of metal, sometimes ceramic or clay, with a tight-fitting lid. The origin of Dutch ovens as cooking vessels dates back hundreds of years. They were used extensively by cooks around the world to prepare a wide variety of food. They're still commonly used from the Australian outback to the rangelands of North America. They've stood the test of time and are widely used in the outdoors because the ones made of cast iron are more or less indestructible, plus easy to use and very versatile. Also, they're really handy around the kitchen and can be used on stovetops and in the oven. You can use a Dutch oven to cook soup, stews, pot roasts, fish, chicken, and even bread, buns and biscuits—practically anything you might desire, if you have the time and patience.

During a roundup or cattle drive, a sooty Dutch oven would rest on a bed of embers in place of a kitchen range or hang on a metal tripod or spit over a campfire. Dutch ovens are great for outdoor cooking because they withstand high heat well and distribute and hold the heat efficiently. Cast iron pots with feet and loop handles are ideal for either sitting right on top of hot embers or suspending from a tripod over a campfire. However, cast iron is quite heavy and not easy to carry long distances. In that case, lighter weight metal pots and pans may be preferable, although they're less durable than cast iron and won't last as long. But weight was not a serious issue during roundups and cattle drives, when Dutch ovens were packed in the hold of a chuckwagon.

The most common size of Dutch oven today is the 12-inch, but they also come in 5, 8, 10, 14 and 16-inch varieties. Briquettes are best for heating your oven but you can also use the wood of a campfire. Most recipes cooked in a Dutch oven require heat from above as well as below, so you have to put briquettes (or wood) on the lid of the oven as well as around its base. As a general rule to reach 325°F, you take as many briquettes as the diameter of your oven and add 3 briquettes to the top and subtract 3 for the base. So if you have a 12-inch oven, you'll need 15 briquettes on the lid and 9 around the base. For every additional briquette you add to the lid and base, you will increase the temperature in the oven by 25°F. Of course all Dutch ovens are slightly different, so you may have to play around a little until you find what works best for your particular oven.

Treated properly, a Dutch oven can last for ages, and many have been passed down through the generations. Metal Dutch ovens can rust if not stored properly; they should be coated with a light film of oil (not too much or it could turn rancid before the oven is used again) then placed back in their box or bag with a folded piece of paper towel tucked the lid, propping it up slightly so that air can circulate inside the oven.

Slow Cooker Elk Roast

Meat was in short supply on cattle drives, with cows usually being butchered only if they were unable to make the long journey, so cowboys kept an eye out for wild game. Many a cowboy enjoyed dining on elk back in the day. Elk are members of the deer family; their meat is considered to be "venison," a term which also includes caribou, deer and moose. Elk are primarily grazers, not unlike cattle, but elk meat is very lean. The secret to cooking venison is to cook the meat slowly at a relatively low heat; a slow cooker or Dutch oven is ideal for preparing elk roasts, particularly for older animals. This elk pot roast recipe is made all the more tasty with the addition of thyme and savoury. Serve it with fresh crusty bread.

Elk roast (3 lbs., 1.4 kg)	1	1
Salt, to taste		
Pepper, to taste		
Large onion, cut in quarters	1	1
Prepared beef or vegetable broth	2 cups	500 mL
Ground thyme	1/8 tsp.	0.5 mL
Ground savory	1/8 tsp.	0.5 mL
Large potatoes, cut in quarters	4	4
Large carrots, chopped	6	6
Flour	2 tbsp.	30 mL

Place elk roast in a slow cooker or dutch oven and sprinkle with salt and pepper to taste. Add onion, broth and herbs. Cook on High for 3 to 4 hours, for a slow cooker or in a 325°F (160°C) oven for about 1 1/2 to 2 hours for a Dutch oven.

Add potatoes and carrots, and continue to cook for another 2 hours in a slow cooker or 1 hour in a Dutch oven, until meat and vegetables are tender. Add flour and stir until sauce is thickened. Serves 5.

1 serving: 600 Calories; 4.5 g Total Fat (1 g Mono, 1 g Poly, 1.5 g Sat); 150 mg Cholesterol; 66 g Carbohydrate (7 g Fibre, 8 g Sugar); 71 g Protein; 510 mg Sodium

꧁꧂ To cook this dish outdoors in a cast iron or aluminum Dutch oven, place 9 briquettes under its base and 15 on the lid.

 When you give a lesson in meanness to a critter or a person, don't be surprised if they learn their lesson.

Veni Stew

Cowboys will be the first to say they enjoy a meal of comfort food, and a stew featuring venison would fit the bill. One of the "safest" ways to prepare venison is in a stew, especially if the animal is old and the meat wasn't aged properly. Young big game animals are naturally tender and do not need to be aged whereas mature big game animals are best aged at least one week, preferably two. If a big game animal was cared for properly in the field, it will not have a "gamey" flavour. Regardless, cooking the cubed meat in a stew will make it tender enough to cut with a fork. With the addition of brown sugar and tomatoes, the stew will have a somewhat sweet taste.

Venison stewing meat	2 lbs.	900 g
Salt	1/2 tsp.	2 mL
Pepper	1/2 tsp.	2 mL
All-purpose flour	1/4 cup	60 mL
Butter (or hard margarine)	3 tbsp.	45 mL
Medium onions, chopped	2	2
Brown sugar, packed	1 tsp.	5 mL
Garlic powder	1/2 tsp.	2 mL
Water or beef broth	4 cups	1 L
Medium tomatoes, diced	4	4
Sliced mushrooms	1 cup	250 mL

Season venison with salt and pepper. Dredge meat in flour.

Heat a skillet over medium, and add butter, onion, brown sugar and garlic powder. Cook for 5 minutes, until onions soften. Add meat and cook for 5 more minutes.

Put meat mixture into a stew pot or Dutch oven. Add water or beef broth. Stir in tomatoes and mushrooms, and simmer for about 1 hour until slightly reduced. Serves 5.

1 serving: 340 Calories; 12 g Total Fat (3 g Mono, 1.5 g Poly, 6 g Sat); 170 mg Cholesterol; 15 g Carbohydrate (2 g Fibre, 6 g Sugar); 44 g Protein; 380 mg Sodium

Oil all the wheels on your wagon, not just the squeaky one.

Grilled Venison Burgers

Grilled ground venison, particularly from elk and moose, is very flavourful. Most people make the mistake of over-cooking venison—it's lean and should be cooked slowly at a medium/low heat—but ground venison is a bit more forgiving. This simple recipe is easy to prepare but will make you look like a superstar!

Ground venison	2 lbs.	900 g
Salt	1/2 tsp.	2 mL
Pepper	1/2 tsp.	2 mL
Hamburger buns	8	8
Cheese slices	8	8
Bacon, fried crisp	1 lb.	454 g
Avocados, peeled and sliced	2	2
Red tomatoes, thinly sliced	2	2
Red onion, thinly sliced	1	1
Romaine lettuce leaves, washed	8	8

Fashion 8 equal-sized patties out of venison and place them on a baking sheet. Season with salt and pepper. Preheat grill to medium and place patties on grill. Cook until desired doneness, about 4 to 5 minutes per side for medium-rare, longer for well done.

Put your cooked patties inside hamburger buns and top with cheese slice, bacon, avocado, tomato, onion and lettuce. Serves 8.

1 serving: 730 Calories; 48 g Total Fat (18 g Mono, 5 g Poly 17 g Sat); 150 mg Cholesterol; 3.1 g Carbohydrate (6 g Fibre, 5 g Sugar); 43 g Protein; 960 mg Sodium

*Never approach a bull from the front,
a horse from the rear or a fool from any direction.*

Pan-fried Trout

A meal of grilled trout in the great outdoors is a fine way to cap a day's outing. Pan-sized trout are notoriously delicious. When the opportunity arose, it was not uncommon for a camp cook to catch some trout from nearby streams as a break from standard meals. Grilled in bacon drippings, the trout would be crispy and flavourful. In this recipe, we've breaded the trout with cornmeal and replaced the traditional bacon drippings with butter. Delicious!

Trout fillets (1 lb., 454 g), skin and any small bones removed	4	4
Cornmeal	1 cup	250 mL
All-purpose flour	2 tbsp.	30 mL
Salt	1/8 tsp.	0.5 mL
Pepper	1/8 tsp.	0.5 mL
Butter (or hard margarine)	6 tbsp.	90 mL

Rinse trout and pat dry.

Combine next 4 ingredients in a large resealable bag. Add fillets, 1 at a time, and toss until coated.

Melt butter in a large frying pan on medium. Add fillets. Cook for 4 to 5 minutes per side until fish flakes easily when tested with a fork. Serves 4.

1 serving: 634 Calories; 31 g Total Fat (8 g Mono, 3 g Poly, 17 g Sat); 162 mg Cholestrol; 46 g Carbohydate (1 g Fibre, 5 g Sugar); 39 g Protein; 404 mg Sodium

🍃 *Cussing at a range cook is
as risky as branding a mule's tail.*

Campfire Smoked Trout

This is a modern-day cowboy recipe that will have folks coming back for seconds. Marinated trout that are grilled over a smoking campfire are a real treat. While this recipe features wood chips, you can also use needles from evergreen trees to impart a smoky flavour to the trout. The secret is to have a large bed of red hot coals when it is time to cook. Also be sure that the grill is adjusted to the proper height above the campfire so that the trout are cooked thoroughly. Serve with a squeeze of lemon juice and horseradish.

Water	2 cups	500 mL
Lemon juice	2 tbsp.	30 mL
Garlic cloves, sliced	5	5
Shallots, sliced	4	4
Salt	2 tbsp.	30 mL
Sugar	2 tbsp.	30 mL
Chopped dill	2 tbsp.	30 mL
Rainbow trout fillets (10 to 12 inches [25 to 30 cm] each)	6	6
Wood chips, soaked for 4 hours and drained	2 cups	500 mL

Combine first 7 ingredients in a medium bowl. Place trout in a shallow baking dish and pour marinade over top. Marinate trout in a cooler or refrigerator for up to 1/2 hour.

Build a charcoal or briquette fire on one side of your grill and place a shallow pan of water in other half. When coals are hot, scatter wet wood chips on top of coals, which will produce large billows of smoke. Remove trout from marinade and place on grill over pan of water. Discard remaining marinade. Place lid or cover over grill to trap smoke inside. Cook for about 30 minutes (depending on amount of smoke). Serves 6.

1 serving: 250 Calories; 9 g Total Fat (2.5 g Mono, 3 g Poly, 2.5 g Sat); 105 mg Cholesterol; 4 g Carbohydrate (0 g Fibre, 2 g Sugar); 37 g Protein; 840 mg Sodium

Easy Grouse in a Pan

When possible, cowboys would bag a grouse so the camp cook could add some variety to the menu. Grouse have very little fat, so they should always be cooked slowly at a low to medium heat, preferably in a covered skillet when done over a campfire so they don't dry out. This simple recipe brings out the best in the natural flavour of grouse.

Olive oil	3 tbsp.	45 mL
Flour	1/4 cup	60 mL
Salt	1/2 tsp.	2 mL
Pepper	1/2 tsp.	2 mL
Grouse breasts, halved	6	6

Prepare your campfire and establish a thick bed of coals. Heat olive oil in a large cast-iron pan.

In a medium bowl, mix flour, salt and pepper. Roll grouse pieces in flour. Lay grouse pieces in pan and cook for about 5 minutes on each side until meat is fully cooked. Serves 6.

1 serving: 320 Calories; 13 g Total Fat (7 g Mono, 1.5 g Poly, 3 g Sat); 105 mg Cholesterol; 4 g Carbohydrate (0 g Fibre, 0 g Sugar); 45 g Protein; 260 mg Sodium

 *Do it right or get off the horse.*

Saucy Roast Duck

Farm and ranch families have a long history of waterfowl hunting. Wild ducks were and still are considered a real treat, particularly chunky grain-fed mallards that are taken late in the hunting season. Wild ducks are very lean compared to domestic ducks, so they should always be cooked slowly at a low to medium heat. This recipe packs a bit of heat, which complements the robust flavour of waterfowl. Serve with mashed potatoes and your favourite fresh veggies.

Small onion, chopped	1	1
Garlic clove, minced	1	1
Butter (or hard margarine)	1 cup	250 mL
Ketchup	1/2 cup	125 mL
Lemon juice	1 1/2 tbsp.	22 mL
Worcestershire sauce	1 tbsp.	15 mL
Hot pepper sauce	1/2 tsp.	2 mL
Salt	1/2 tsp.	2 mL
Pepper	1/2 tsp.	2 mL
Duck, rinsed and patted dry (2 to 3 lbs., 900 g to 1.4 kg)	1	1

Combine first 9 ingredients in a small pot. Cook, stirring, on medium heat for about 5 minutes, until butter is melted and ingredients blend.

Split duck in half lengthwise, and place in a roasting pan breast up. Pour sauce over top. Cook in 350°F (175°C) oven for approximately 2 hours until juices run clear, basting every 15 minutes or so. Let stand for 5 minutes before serving. Serves 4.

1 serving: 930 Calories; 81 g Total Fat (27 g Mono, 6 g Poly, 41 g Sat); 305 mg Cholesterol; 11 g Carbohydrate (0 g Fibre, 10 g Sugar); 40 g Protein; 1180 mg Sodium

Canada Goose Stew

Canada geese, like ducks, tend to be quite lean compared to their domestic counterparts and should be cooked in a manner that doesn't dry them out, such as in a slow cooker or Dutch oven. This particular recipe brings out the best flavour in geese and will tenderize even rather large, older birds, which might be a wee bit on the tough side.

Goose breasts, halved	2	2
Red onion, chopped	1	1
Red pepper, chopped	1	1
Green peppers, chopped	2	2
Carrots, chopped	2	2
Garlic cloves, minced	2	2
Can of diced tomatoes (28 oz., 796 mL)	1	1
Sliced mushrooms	1 cup	250 mL
Salt	1/2 tsp.	2 mL
Pepper	1/2 tsp.	2 mL

Cut goose into bite-sized stew pieces and place in a slow cooker or Dutch oven. Add remaining ingredients, stir, and cook on Low for 7 to 8 hours for a slow cooker or in a 325°F (160°C) oven for about 1 1/2 to 2 hours for a Dutch oven. Serves 4.

1 serving: 450 Calories; 29 g Total Fat (13 g Mono, 4 g Poly, 7 g Sat); 110 mg Cholesterol; 20 g Carbohydrate (4 g Fibre, 12 g Sugar); 29 g Protein; 1040 mg Sodium

To cook this dish outdoors in a cast iron or aluminum Dutch oven, place 9 briquettes under its base and 15 on the lid.

Every trail has a few puddles in it.

Rodeos

🖋 *The only good reason to ride a bull is to meet a nurse.*

A cowboy's life has always revolved around horses and cattle. Back in the day, rodeos were held as competitions between local cowboys to gauge their riding and roping skills, as well as their steer wrestling. The early rodeos of the 1820s and 1830s in the western United States and northern Mexico were informal events. They went public between 1890 and 1910 and were sometimes combined with Wild West shows featuring stars such as Buffalo Bill Cody and Annie Oakley. The first official rodeo in Canada was held in Raymond, Alberta, in 1902. The first Canadian Finals Rodeo took place in Edmonton in 1974. The event now offers one of the richest purses in Canadian rodeo, worth over $1 million dollars in 2014. The first Calgary Stampede was in 1912 and has grown ever since, with a purse of over $2 million in 2014.

There's little argument that Hugh Dempsey's assertion is correct in *The Golden Age of the Canadian Cowboy* (1995) that "The most enduring and positive depiction of the cowboy through the years has come through rodeos." As he points out, a cowboy's riding ability and skill with a rope are equally at home on the ranch or rodeo ground. A cowboy's lariat is his calling card, even in modern times.

Most rural rodeos feature mainly "local" cowboys who travel the provincial rodeo circuit. In contrast, exhibitions and rodeos in large towns and cities, such as the Calgary Stampede, Edmonton's Canadian Finals Rodeo and the Ponoka Stampede, showcase national and international contestants who compete for large cash prizes. Over time, lots of side events have piggybacked their way onto rodeos, which sometimes take on a carnival atmosphere with large parades, midways, grandstand shows, chuckwagon races, shooting events, food courts and beer gardens, agricultural fairs, casinos, country and western bands and singers, talent shows and evening fireworks displays.

Rodeos have come a long way over the years, and they've evolved into big ticket entertainment events with a large and loyal following in both Canada and the United States.

Creamed Spinach ✓

Greens did not make up a large part of the cowboy diet on the trail because there was no way to keep them fresh, but many cooks planted their own gardens back at the ranch, and some clever chuckwagon cooks even planted small gardens along the trail so that a variety of hearty vegetables would be available for harvest the next time the cattle drive passed through the area. Creamed spinach is a go-to side dish for many cowboy recipes, including steaks, roasts and fried chicken. This easy-to-make recipe is always a family favourite, and the nutmeg gives the spinach a subtle sweetness.

Butter (or hard margarine)	1/3 cup	75 mL
All-purpose flour	1/3 cup	75 mL
Salt	1 1/4 tsp.	6 mL
Ground nutmeg	1/4 tsp.	1 mL
Pepper	1/4 tsp.	1 mL
Milk	2 1/2 cups	625 mL
Boxes of frozen chopped spinach, (10 oz., 300 g) thawed and squeezed dry	3	3

Melt butter in a medium saucepan on medium. Add next 4 ingredients. Cook, stirring, for 1 minute.

Slowly add milk, stirring constantly, until smooth. Cook, stirring, for 5 to 10 minutes until boiling and thickened. Reduce heat to medium-low.

Add spinach. Cook, stirring, for about 5 minutes, until heated through. Serves 4.

1 serving: 160 Calories; 9 g Total Fat (2 g Mono, 0.5 g Poly, 5 g Sat); 25 mg Cholesterol; 14 g Carbohydrate (4 g Fibre, 5 g Sugar); 9 g Protein; 910 mg Sodium

Don't go milking your neighbour's cow.

Creamed Onions

This recipe is a tribute to the vast number of cowboys in Canada who hailed from England. In the late 19th and early 20th centuries, many young men of noble blood were essentially paid by their family to cross the pond and settle in British colonies. Many of these so-called Remittance Men found their way to western Canada to try their hand at becoming cowboys. They brought with them some of their favourite dishes from home, including creamed onions, a traditional English dish that has gained popularity in Canada and the U.S., particularly at Christmas and Thanksgiving. This dish is often served alongside a main course of roast, chicken, turkey or steak.

Water	4 cups	1 L
Salt	1 tsp.	5 mL
White pearl onions	1 1/2 cups	375 mL
Butter (or hard margarine)	1/3 cup	75 mL
All-purpose flour	1/3 cup	75 mL
Half-and-half cream	3 cups	750 mL
Pepper	1/2 tsp.	2 mL
Salt	1/4 tsp.	1 mL
Ground allspice	1/4 tsp.	1 mL
Fresh bread crumbs	1 cup	250 mL
Chopped fresh sage	1 tbsp.	15 mL
Chopped fresh thyme	2 tsp.	10 mL
Butter (or hard margarine), melted	3 tbsp.	45 mL

Bring water and first amount of salt to a boil in a large pot. Peel onions and drop into boiling salted water. Reduce to a simmer and cook, covered, for about 20 minutes until tender. Drain onions, reserving the liquid, and transfer onions to a greased 2 quart (2 L) baking dish.

Melt butter in a medium saucepan over medium-low heat. Add flour and cook, stirring for about 1 minute, to make a roux.

Add cream, stirring constantly, until mixture is thickened, about 5 minutes. If mixture is too thick, add some reserved onion water until it becomes a nice consistency. Stir in pepper, second amount of salt and allspice. Pour sauce over onions.

Combine last 4 ingredients in a small bowl and sprinkle over onions. Bake on middle rack of 350°F (175°C) oven for about 30 minutes until golden and bubbling. Let it rest for 5 minutes before serving. Serves 6.

1 serving: 450 Calories; 30 g Total Fat (8 g Mono, 1 g Poly, 19 g Sat); 85 mg Cholesterol; 41 g Carbohydrate (1 g Fibre, 4 g Sugar); 8 g Protein; 690 mg Sodium

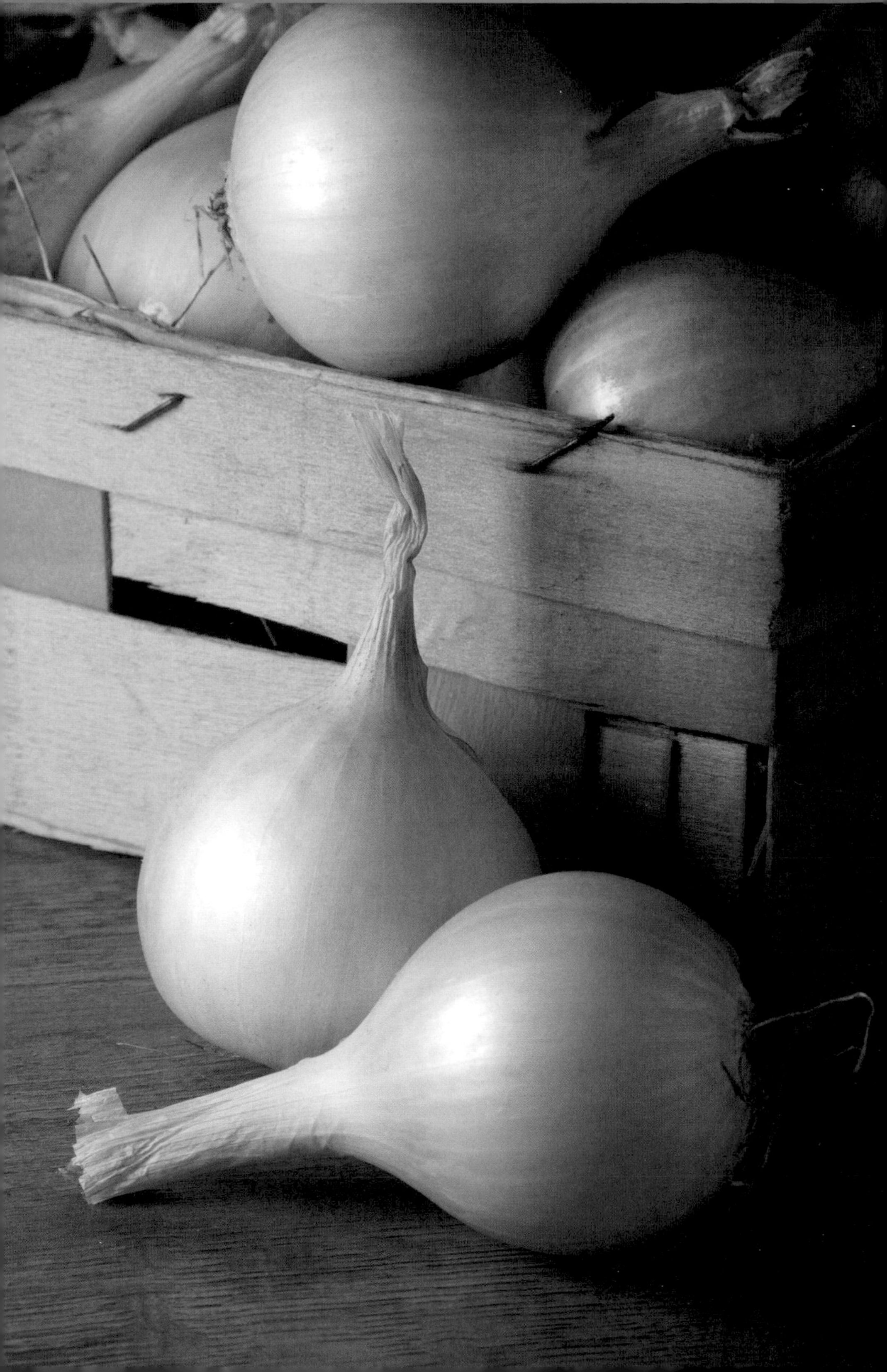

Grilled Corn

Cowboys and corn seem to go hand in hand, and while there are many ways to prepare corn on the cob, one of the traditional ways is still the best—grilled over the red-hot coals of a campfire. Once the husks are removed and the cobs have been brushed with butter, salt and pepper, they won't last long!

Medium corncobs in husks	6	6
Butter (or hard margarine), softened	1/2 cup	125 mL
Salt, to taste		
Pepper, to taste		

Pull husks down to end of corncobs, leaving them attached to the cobs. Remove and discard silk. Spread butter evenly over cobs. Sprinkle with salt and pepper. Bring husks back up to cover cobs. Preheat barbecue to medium. Place cobs on ungreased grill and close lid. Cook for about 12 minutes, turning cobs a quarter turn every 3 minutes, until tender. Remove and discard husks. Serves 6.

1 serving: 170 Calories; 11 g Total Fat (3 g Mono, 1 g Poly, 7 g Sat); 25 mg Cholesterol; 17 g Carbohydrate (2 g Fibre, 3 g Sugar); 3 g Protein; 85 mg Sodium

Creamed corn was a staple for cowboys on the range who had to fend for themselves come dinner time. Along with dried meat, cowboys carried dried corn in their saddlebags, which they would rehydrate with boiling water, stirring until the corn's natural starches turned the dish creamy.

Warm Potato Salad

Chuckwagon cooks relied on hardy vegetables that could take some abuse in the back of the wagon and still be in good enough shape to use in a meal. Potatoes fit the bill. This potato salad recipe has a long history with farm and ranch families, especially in Canada. It was traditionally cooked in a skillet over a campfire or on a stovetop but could also be baked as a casserole. Parboiling the spuds allows them to cook quickly in a heated barbecue and absorb the full flavour of the other ingredients.

Medium potatoes, cut into 3/4 inch (2 cm) cubes	4	4
Bacon slices, cooked crisp and crumbled	4	4
Finely chopped onion	1/3 cup	75 mL
Finely chopped celery	1/4 cup	60 mL
Mayonnaise (not salad dressing)	1/3 cup	75 mL
Sour cream	1/4 cup	60 mL
Apple cider vinegar	3 tbsp.	45 mL
Sugar	1 tbsp.	15 mL
Garlic cloves, minced (or 1/4 tsp., 1 mL, powder)	1	1
Dry mustard	1 tsp.	5 mL
Salt	1/2 tsp.	2 mL
Pepper	1/4 tsp.	1 mL

Place potatoes in a large pot with enough water to cover. Bring to a boil and cook until tender, about 15 minutes. Drain and transfer to a large bowl.

Add bacon, onion and celery. Place mixture in centre of a 16-inch (40 cm) length of heavy-duty (or double layer of regular) foil.

Combine remaining 8 ingredients in a small bowl. Drizzle over potato mixture. Bring up 2 long sides of foil and seal with double fold. Fold sides in to enclose potato mixture. Preheat gas barbecue to high. Reduce heat to medium-low. Place packet on ungreased grill. Close lid. Cook for about 20 minutes, turning occasionally, until hot. Serves 4.

1 serving: 520 Calories; 34 g Total Fat (16 g Mono, 6 g Poly, 9 g Sat); 40 mg Cholesterol; 43 g Carbohydrate (4 g Fibre, 6 g Sugar); 10 g Protein; 760 mg Sodium

Cowboy Caviar

Loaded with corn, black beans and tomato, this hearty salad would have fit right in on the plates of vaqueros in the American southwest. It is our homage to Texas Caviar, a salad made popular in Texas in the 1950s by Helen Corbitt, a famous food consultant for Neiman Marcus. In place of the black beans, the original salad featured black-eyed peas, or "Athens cowpeas," which were a Texas specialty and were grown in record numbers in the town of Athens, Texas. At the time, Athens enjoyed the title of Black-eyed Pea Capital of the World. They've scaled back production somewhat in recent times, but Texas Caviar is still hugely popular throughout the state.

Can of black beans (19 oz., 540 mL), drained and rinsed	1	1
Chopped red onion	1/2 cup	125 mL
Chopped fresh cilantro	1 tbsp.	15 mL
Diced jalapeño pepper, ribs and seeds removed	1 tbsp.	15 mL
Lime juice	1 tbsp.	15 mL
Ground cumin	1/4 tsp.	1 mL
Chili powder	1/4 tsp.	1 mL
Large tomato, seeded and chopped	1	1
Garlic clove, minced	1	1
Can of kernel corn (12 oz., 341 mL), drained	1	1
Salt	1/2 tsp.	2 mL

Combine all 11 ingredients in a medium bowl. Cover and chill for at least 2 hours to blend flavours. Serves 8.

1 serving: 110 Calories; 1 g Total Fat (trace Mono, 0 g Poly, 0 g Sat); 0 mg Cholesterol; 20 g Carbohydrate (6 g Fibre, 4 g Sugar); 6 g Protein; 370 mg Sodium

Quick Slaw

The cowboy diet was typically heavy on meat and beans and light on vegetables, especially a few weeks into a cattle drive. Any veggies that made it into the chuckwagon had to be hardy enough to survive the rigours of the trail. Whereas delicate greens like lettuce or spinach would have been quickly reduced to an inedible sludge, cabbage had more staying power. Cooks would often whip up a large batch of coleslaw before heading out, loading it into the wagon where it would keep for a few weeks, if stored properly. Traditional cowboy coleslaws would have been vinegar based, but we've added a touch of mayonnaise to this dish for a little added flair.

Small head green cabbage, thinly sliced	1	1
Red cabbage, thinly sliced	1/4 cup	60 mL
Medium carrot, shredded	1	1
Mayonnaise	2/3 cup	150 mL
Sugar	3 tbsp.	45 mL
Salt	3/4 tsp.	4 mL
Celery seed	3/4 tsp.	4 mL
White vinegar	3 tbsp.	45 mL
Mustard	3/4 tsp.	4 mL
White pepper, to taste		

Combine green and red cabbage and carrot in a large bowl and set aside.

Combine remaining ingredients in a small bowl and mix well. Pour part of dressing into cabbage mixture to moisten. Refrigerate until ready to serve. Serve additional dressing on the side. Serves 4.

1 serving: 380 Calories; 27 g Total Fat (16 g Mono, 8 g Poly, 2.5 g Sat); 15 mg Cholesterol; 27 g Carbohydrate (5 g Fibre, 18 g Sugar); 4 g Protein; 770 mg Sodium

Braised Red Cabbage with Apple and Bacon

Cooks on farms and ranches often make this savoury and delicious dish to celebrate holidays, especially as a side dish with roasted pork or turkey. It also goes well with waterfowl. There's just something about the tangy aroma of braised red cabbage that catches one's attention.

Thick slice bacon, diced	1/4 cup	60 mL
Brown sugar	3 tbsp.	45 mL
White onions, diced	2	2
Medium head red cabbage, shredded and soaked in cold water	1	1
Apple cider vinegar	1/4 cup	60 mL
Red wine	1 cup	250 mL
Granny Smith apples, chopped	2	2
Fennel seeds	1/2 tsp.	2 mL
Salt	1/2 tsp.	2 mL
Red wine	2/3 cup	150 mL

Heat a Dutch oven over medium and fry bacon until fat begins to melt. Add brown sugar and continue to cook until bacon reaches a deep golden brown.

Lower heat to medium-low and add onions, stirring occasionally. Cook for 20 to 30 minutes until onion turns brown and caramelizes.

Drain cabbage and pat dry. Stir cabbage and vinegar into onion mixture. Add first amount of wine, apple, fennel seeds and salt. Mix well, and simmer, covered, for 1 1/2 hours. Check occasionally, adding second amount of wine to prevent sticking, if needed. Remove from heat and allow to rest for 5 minutes before serving. Serves 8.

1 serving: 230 Calories; 9 g Total Fat (4 g Mono, 1 g Poly, 3 g Sa t); 15 mg Cholesterol; 25 g Carbohydrate (4 g Fibre, 17 g Sugar); 4 g Protein; 340 mg Sodium

Fast Bean Salad

A busy farm or ranch wife will often serve a bean salad at suppertime for hungry cowboys because it's tasty and rich in protein. This recipe is easy to make and can accompany all manner of main dishes, particularly steaks, pork chops and fried chicken. It is also a great salad for an outdoor meal because it keeps well out of the fridge.

Frozen cut green beans	1 cup	250 mL
Can of mixed beans (19 oz., 540 mL), rinsed and drained	1	1
Chopped celery	1/2 cup	125 mL
Chopped green onion	1/2 cup	125 mL
Chopped red pepper	1/2 cup	125 mL
Fat-free Italian dressing	1/4 cup	60 mL

Pour water into a small saucepan until about 1 inch (2.5 cm) deep and bring to a boil. Reduce heat to medium and add green beans. Boil gently, covered, for about 2 minutes until tender-crisp. Immediately plunge into ice water in a medium bowl. Let stand for about 5 minutes until cold. Drain.

Meanwhile combine next 4 ingredients in a large bowl. Drizzle with dressing. Add green beans and toss until coated. Serves 4.

1 serving: 190 Calories; 5 g Total Fat (0 g Mono, 0 g Poly, 1 g Sat); 0 mg Cholesterol; 28 g Carbohydrate (8 g Fibre, 4 g Sugar); 9 g Protein; 520 mg Sodium

Another type of "salad" that cowboys back in the day would have been familiar with, but that might not have much appeal for modern palates, is gelatin salad. And we're not talking about the fruity jellied salads that were popular a few decades ago. We're talking boiling the jaw bone of a large animal, often a moose, with some herbs and spices, cutting the meat from the bone and finely slicing it, then storing it in jars covered with the boiling liquid. As the liquid cooled, it would gel, preserving the meat. The end result would be gelatin salad that could be eaten as-is or served on biscuits, bread or crackers.

Carrot and Beet Salad

Carrots and beets are two other hardy vegetables that would have been grown in private gardens on ranches across the country. They could be stored for lengthy periods, providing fresh veggies long after the growing season ended, and they were hardy enough to last a while on the chuckwagon, should the cook choose to include them.

Olive oil	1/4 cup	60 mL
Lemon juice	3 tbsp.	45 mL
Liquid honey	2 tbsp.	30 mL
Salt	1/4 tsp.	1 mL
Pepper	1/4 tsp.	1 mL
Coarsely grated carrot	2 cups	500 mL
Can of whole baby beets, drained (14 oz., 398 mL) and diced	1	1
Chopped fresh mint	2 tsp.	10 mL

For the dressing, whisk first 5 ingredients in a small bowl until smooth. Set aside.

Put carrot and beet into a medium bowl. Toss. Drizzle with dressing. Toss until coated. Sprinkle with mint. Serves 6.

1 serving: 140 Calories; 9 g Total Fat (7 g Mono, 1 g Poly, 1.5 g Sat); 0 mg Cholesterol; 15 g Carbohydrate (2 g Fibre, 11 g Sugar); 1 g Protein; 250 mg Sodium

Creamy Cucumbers

If there ever was a favourite traditional recipe for a cucumber salad, it would have to be creamy cucumbers, always popular on farms and ranches. Cowboys would enjoy a chilled cucumber salad on a hot day after mending fences, tending cattle and doing other farm chores. This dish pairs well with beef, chicken and pork main courses.

Medium English cucumbers, with peel	2	2
Light sour cream	2/3 cup	150 mL
White vinegar	1 tbsp.	15 mL
Small onion, thinly sliced	1	1
Chopped fresh dill (or 1 1/2 tsp., 7 mL, dill weed)	2 tbsp.	30 mL
Salt	1/2 tsp.	2 mL
Pepper	1/8 tsp.	0.5 mL
Sugar	2 tsp.	10 mL

Draw a fork down length of cucumbers all around, piercing peel. Thinly slice into a medium bowl.

Combine remaining 7 ingredients in a small bowl. Add to cucumber and toss until well coated. Serves 5.

1 serving: 80 Calories; 3.5 g Total Fat (1 g Mono, 0 g Poly, 2 g Sat); 10 mg Cholesterol; 10 g Carbohydrate (trace Fibre, 4 g Sugar); 2 g Protein; 260 mg Sodium

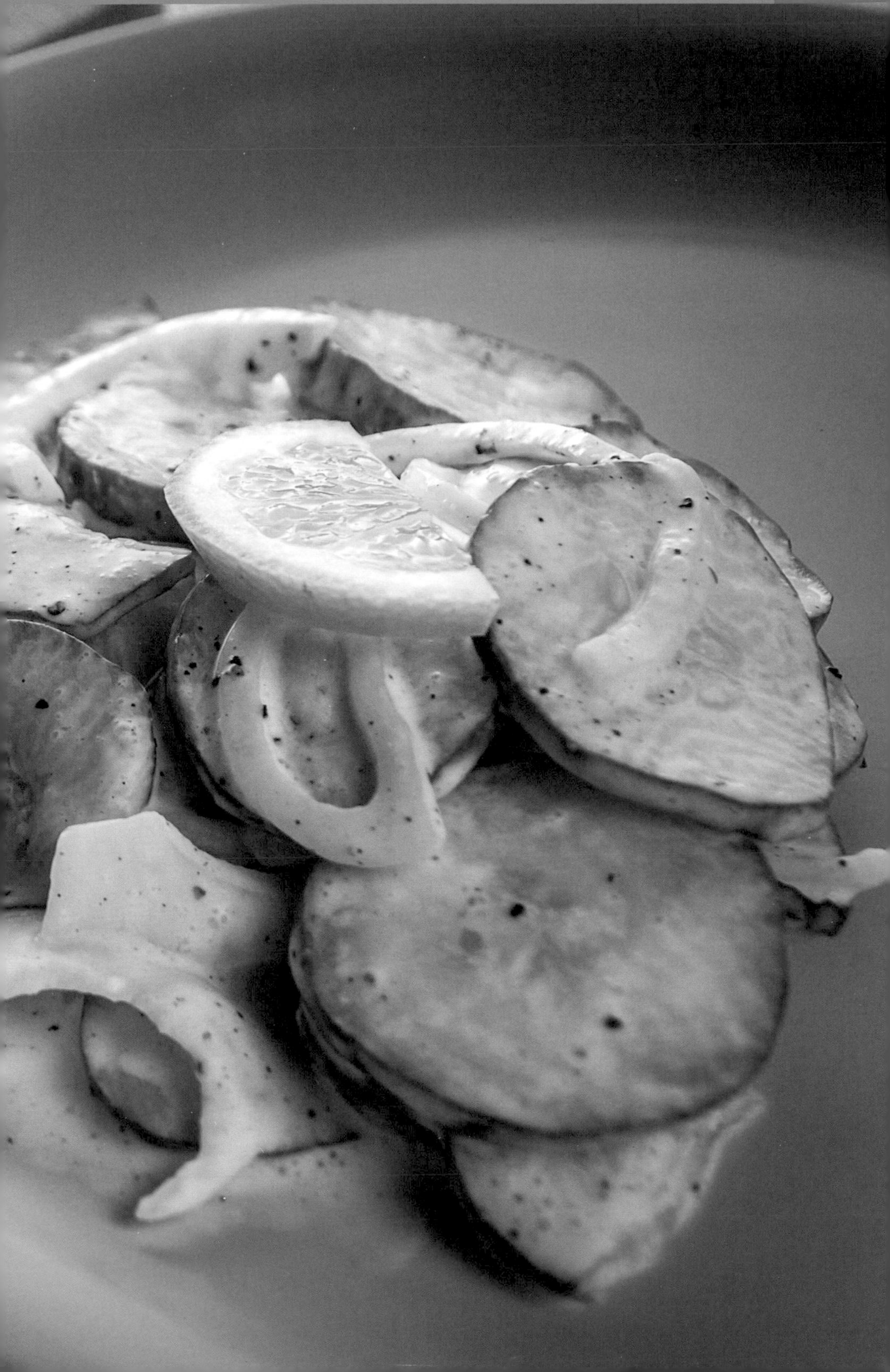

Ranch Dressing

While cowboys are not known as vegans, they do enjoy a garden salad from time to time, and ranch dressing would be high on the list of their go-to dressings. Ranch dressing has been the best-selling salad dressing flavour in the U.S. since 1992. This popular salad dressing has it roots on the Hidden Valley Guest Ranch near Santa Barbara, California. The ranch owners made a dressing with herbs, spices and buttermilk that became popular with their guests. Currently, the Hidden Valley brand appears on several varieties of prepared dressing in supermarkets across Canada and the U.S. Ranch dressing has long been popular as a vegetable dip and as a dip for potato chips, as well as a tasty salad dressing.

Mayonnaise (not salad dressing)	1 cup	250 mL
Granulated garlic or onion powder	1 tsp.	5 mL
Chopped chives or green onions, plus extra for garnish	2 tsp.	10 mL
Chopped parsley, plus extra for garnish	2 tsp.	10 mL
Garlic powder	1/2 tsp.	2 mL
Salt	1/2 tsp.	2 mL
Freshly ground black pepper	1/2 tsp.	2 mL
Dried oregano	1/2 tsp.	2 mL
Dried thyme	1/2 tsp.	2 mL
Buttermilk (regular or low fat)	1 1/2 cups	375 mL

To make the dressing, blend together all ingredients in a bowl. Keeps for 2 weeks in the refrigerator. Makes 2 2/3 cups (650 mL).

2 tbsp. (30 mL): *80 Calories; 7 g Total Fat (4.5 g Mono, 2 g Poly, 1 g Sat); trace Cholesterol; 1 g Carbohydrate (0 g Fibre, 1 g Sugar); trace Protein; 130 mg Sodium*

A stubborn horse walks behind you, an impatient horse walks in front of you, but a noble companion walks beside you.

The Calgary Stampede

The Calgary Stampede has become one of Canada's most iconic tourist attractions. It has wide appeal to folks having an interest in cowboys and ranching, western events, midway exhibits and attractions.

The Calgary Stampede bills itself as "The Greatest Outdoor Show on Earth," no small boast, and it lives up to this tribute. It all started when Guy Weadick, an American entrepreneur, spearheaded the first cowboy rodeo known as "The Stampede" in Calgary from September 2 to 7, 1912. The inaugural event was scheduled after most farmers and ranchers had completed their autumn harvest to boost attendance. Weadick couldn't possibly have pulled off the kickoff Stampede without the financial support of A.E. Cross, A.J. MacLean, Pat Burns and George Lane, the "Big Four" businessmen who, along with Weadick, contributed $100,000 to that first show. They promoted "world titles," which boosted interest and attracted the best cowboys in Canada and the United States.

There was no Calgary Stampede during the four years of World War I. The second Stampede took place in 1919, which was called the Victory Stampede to honour the end of the war. Guy Weadick spearheaded the event again, and it was held annually starting in 1923.

As the saying goes, after 1923, "the rest is history." That year, the name was changed to "The Calgary Exhibition and Stampede," eventually becoming known as simply the Calgary Stampede. Now held each July, the event currently attracts over one million visitors annually, a testament to its popularity. Calgarians let their hair down and kick up their heels to celebrate the Stampede with visitors from around the world. Western dress is the norm, as city folks don blue jeans, a cowboy belt and buckle, cowboy boots, long-sleeved plaid shirts and the signature Calgary Stampede white Stetson, the hallmark of western hospitality.

The action-packed 10-day stampede seems to get better each year. It kicks off with a parade along the streets of downtown Calgary. The whole area reverberates with the sounds of marching bands combined with the trill of bagpipes, the beat of drums and the rhythmic clacking of horse hooves on pavement amid the palpable excitement of the crowd of onlookers. The Calgary Stampede rodeo attracts the

world's top cowboys, who compete for more than $2 million in prize money. It features six events daily: ladies' barrel racing, bareback, tie-down roping, steer wrestling, saddle bronc and bull riding. Then there are the (uniquely) Canadian chuckwagon races in the evening performance, which are guaranteed to put spectators on the edge of their seats. The grandstand show is world class, not unlike an extravagant Las Vegas performance. The midway has a mind-boggling number of rides and attractions.

All and all, just being at the Stampede can be a very moving and rewarding experience. It's a bucket list event for many folks that's not to be missed, and keeps on entertaining millions of people year after year. In June 2013, when floodwaters threatened the Stampede, thousands of volunteers worked with city officials and construction companies around the clock so that it could proceed as usual. T-shirts with the motto "Come Hell or High Water" helped raise funds to ensure success.

Old-fashioned Campfire Bannock

Cowboys have long enjoyed their flatbreads. Bannock is a kind of flatbread that can be cooked over a campfire by wrapping the dough around a tree branch or frying it in a greased skillet. Some cooks add raisins or berries to flavour the bannock, which has long been popular among First Nations and Inuit peoples as well as outdoorsmen and women throughout Canada. Basic bannock can also be made with boiled potatoes added to the dough and is considered especially tasty when eaten fresh after being cooked in lard. Enriched bannock has skim milk and beaten eggs added to the basic ingredients; it should be cooked until it turns golden brown on one side and then turned over to cook the other side.

All-purpose flour	2 cups	500 mL
Baking powder	1 tbsp.	15 mL
Butter	3 tbsp.	45 mL
Salt	1 tsp.	5 mL
Warm water	2/3 cup	150 mL
Cooking oil	1 tbsp.	15 mL

Place flour, baking powder, butter and salt in a large bowl and mix with your hands until dough clumps. Slowly add water and mix until dough softens (you may not use the entire 2/3 cup, 150 mL, water). Let dough rest, covered, for 30 minutes.

Divide dough into quarters and shape each portion into a ball. Flatten with a rolling pin, or your hand, into a disk about 1/2 inch (1 cm) thick. Heat frying pan over medium and add oil. Cook bannock on both sides, turning once, until golden brown. Alternatively, you can forgo the frying pan and simply twist dough around a clean stick and hold over open campfire until golden and crispy. Serves 4.

1 serving: 310 Calories; 9 g Total Fat (2.5 g Mono, 0.5 g Poly, 6 g Sat); 25 mg Cholesterol; 44 g Carbohydrate (2 g Fibre, 0 g Sugar); 7 g Protein; 860 mg Sodium

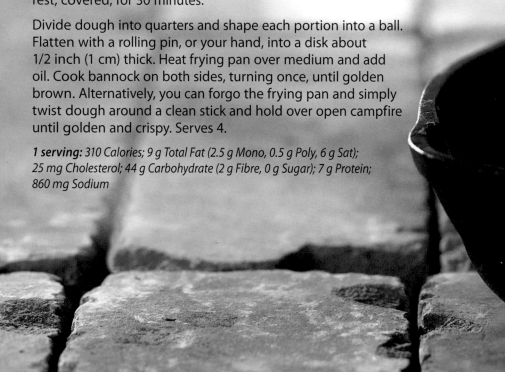

Sourdough Biscuits

Sourdough starter was a prized possession of every chuckwagon cook. With his starter, a cook could whip up sourdough breads, buns and, perhaps most popular, biscuits for his crew. In colder months, cooks were known to take their starter to bed with them so their body heat would keep the starter from freezing.

All-purpose flour	1 1/2 cups	375 mL
Baking powder	2 tsp.	10 mL
Baking soda	1/2 tsp.	2 mL
Salt	1/2 tsp.	2 mL
Cooking oil	1/3 cup	75 mL
Sourdough starter, room temperature, see below	1 cup	250 mL

Measure first 4 ingredients into a medium bowl. Stir well.

Add cooking oil and sourdough starter. Stir to form a ball. Turn dough out onto a floured surface and roll or pat until 3/4 inch (2 cm) thick. Cut into 2 inch (5 cm) rounds. Arrange on ungreased baking sheet. Bake in 425°F (220°C) oven for about 12 minutes. Makes 16 biscuits.

1 biscuit: 110 Calories; 4.5 g Total Fat (3 g Mono, 1.5 g Poly, 0 g Sat); 0 mg Cholesterol; 15 g Carbohydrate (trace Fibre, 0 g Sugar); 2 g Protein; 150 mg Sodium

Quick Sourdough Starter

Water	1 cup	250 mL
All-purpose flour	1 cup	250 mL
Active dry yeast	1/2 tsp.	2 mL

The night before you plan to make biscuits, mix all 3 ingredients together and set out on a countertop in a draft-free area, allowing starter time to develop. Remaining starter can be left on the counter for future use; it is best stored at 65 to 77°F (18 to 25°C). To strengthen and "feed" starter, add 1/4 cup (60 mL) water and 1/2 cup (125 mL) flour every second day.

 Biscuits played a huge role in the cowboy diet. They were filling, relatively quick and easy to make, and could hold up in a saddlebag better than bread could. The biscuits of old were not the light, fluffy biscuits of today; they were harder and drier. Every chuckwagon cook had his own special (and carefully guarded) recipe, and cowboys would judge his cooking skill by the quality of his biscuits. Shortcomings in his soups, stews and the like could be forgiven as long as he got the biscuits right. Sourdough biscuits were more common on the trail, but back at the ranch, buttermilk biscuits were also popular.

Basic Cornbread

Cornbread wasn't a huge part of the cowboy scene in Canada, but it was essential among vaqueros and cowboys in the southwestern U.S. Much like cowboys on the range in Canada would carry bannock or biscuits to stave off hunger throughout the day, cowboys in the U.S. would carry cornbread.

All-purpose flour	1 1/2 cups	375 mL
Yellow cornmeal	1 cup	250 mL
Sugar	1/2 cup	125 mL
Baking powder	2 tsp.	10 mL
Baking soda	1 tsp.	5 mL
Salt	1/2 tsp.	2 mL
Large egg	1	1
Buttermilk (or soured milk, see Tip, below)	1 cup	250 mL
Butter (or hard margarine), melted	1/4 cup	60 mL

Combine first 6 ingredients in a large bowl. Make a well in centre.

Combine remaining 3 ingredients in a small bowl. Add to well. Spread in a greased 9 x 9 inch (23 x 23 cm) pan. Bake in 350°F (175°C) oven for about 30 minutes until wooden pick inserted in centre comes out clean. Let stand in pan for 5 minutes before removing to wire rack to cool. Serves 12.

1 serving: 190 Calories; 4.5 g Total Fat (1.5 g Mono, 0 g Poly, 3 g Sat); 30 mg Cholesterol; 32 g Carbohydrate (trace Fibre, 9 g Sugar); 4 g Protein; 280 mg Sodium

Tip: To make sour milk, measure 1 tbsp. (15 mL) white vinegar or lemon juice into a 1 cup (250 mL) liquid measure. Add enough milk to make 1 cup (250 mL). Stir and let sit for 1 minute.

Camp Bread

A cowboy can eat only so many biscuits, so cooks would shake things up a little and serve some old-fashioned camp bread alongside a thick stew or plate of beans. For a snack version of camp bread, a cook might add some raisins, sugar or cinnamon to the dough. Camp bread could be fried in a skillet or baked in a Dutch oven; the Dutch oven camp bread would be softer than the fried variety.

Vegetable oil	1/4 cup	60 mL
All-purpose flour	2 cups	500 mL
Baking powder	1 tsp.	5 mL
Salt	1 tsp.	5 mL
Shortening	1 tbsp.	15 mL
Water	3/4 cup	175 mL

Prepare campfire, or preheat grill to medium. Heat oil in large cast-iron skillet or Dutch oven. Mix flour, baking powder and salt in medium bowl. Work in shortening, then add water and mix well. Shape into 6 balls of equal size. Roll 1 ball of dough at a time to 1/8 inch (3 mm) thick rounds. Pan-fry until golden brown. Serves 6.

1 serving: 210 Calories; 7 g Total Fat (3 g Mono, 1.5 g Poly, 1 g Sat); 0 mg Cholesterol; 32 g Carbohydrate (1 g Fibre, 0 g Sugar); 4 g Protein; 440 mg Sodium

Camp bread can trace its roots back to hard tack, a dried cracker-like bread that soldiers carried as provisions during the American Civil War. For a little variety in their bland diet, soldiers would sometimes crush the cake into powder, mix in a little water to form a dough and pan-fry it. The end result would be a fresh flatbread. Modern-day camp bread uses flour and a leavening agent instead of crushed hard tack and is often pan-fried in bacon grease or deep fried in oil or lard.

If a camp cook ain't grouchy, he ain't been cookin' long enough.

Air Buns

*Air buns are popular, sweet dinner rolls that go well with soups and stews.
A yeast bread would have made a nice change from the biscuits that usually
filled a cowboy's plate. This recipe yields a lot of buns, but they keep well and
can always be frozen to be used later. This is a fail-safe recipe that's been around
for ages. Feel free to substitute honey for the white sugar, if you prefer.*

Hot water	4 cups	1 L
Butter (or hard margarine), cut up	1/2 cup	125 mL
Sugar	1/2 cup	125 mL
White vinegar	1 tbsp.	15 mL
Salt	1 tsp.	5 mL
All-purpose flour	4 cups	1 L
Instant yeast (1/4 oz., 8 g)	1	1
All-purpose flour	7 1/2 cups	1.8 L
Butter (or hard margarine), softened	2 tbsp.	30 mL

Combine first 5 ingredients in a large bowl. Stir to melt butter. Cool to
lukewarm.

Combine first amount of flour and yeast in a small bowl. Beat slowly into
wet ingredients until smooth. Work in enough of second amount of flour
until dough pulls away from sides of bowl. Place in greased bowl, turning
once to grease top. Cover with a tea towel. Let stand in oven with light on
and door closed for 1 to 1 1/2 hours until doubled in bulk. Punch dough
down. Cover with tea towel. Let stand in oven with light on and door closed
for 1 hour. Punch dough down and shape into 60 egg-size balls. Place on
greased baking sheets 2 inches (5 cm) apart. Cover with a tea towel. Let
stand in oven with light on and door closed for 3 hours. Bake in 350°F
(175°C) oven for about 20 minutes until golden brown. Turn out onto
racks to cool.

Brush warm tops with butter. Makes 60 buns.

*1 bun: 110 Calories; 2 g Total Fat (0.5 g Mono, 0 g Poly, 1.5 g Sat); 5 mg Cholesterol;
20 g Carbohydrate (trace Fibre, 2 g Sugar); 3 g Protein; 55 mg Sodium*

John Ware and family, circa 1897

Legendary
Canadian Cowboys

John Ware was Canada's most famous black cowboy. Born a slave in the southern U.S. in 1845, Ware gained his freedom near the end of the Civil War and found work on a cattle ranch near Fort Worth, Texas. He came to Alberta in 1882 when he helped drive 3000 head of cattle up through Montana to a ranch west of High River. He soon gained a reputation as a skilled horseman. He was considered one of the best bucking horse riders at the first annual fair and rodeo held in Calgary in 1883, where he won the steer-roping contest. Later on he became one of Canada's top bronc riders. Ware participated in one of the greatest roundups ever in southwestern Alberta in 1885. He was rated as one of Canada's top cowboys in the 1890s. The *Macleod Gazette* said, "The horse is not running on the prairie which John cannot ride." He died on September 14, 1905; while he was cutting a steer from a herd of cattle, his horse stumbled in a badger hole and fell on him, breaking his neck and killing him instantly. He was buried in Calgary where his tombstone overlooks today's Calgary Stampede grounds, a fitting tribute.

Guy Weadick is credited with founding the Calgary Stampede in 1912. Born in New York in 1885, he was a Wild West vaudeville performer who had the vision for a world-class cowboy event in Calgary "as a tribute to the memory of the cowboy," according to Hugh Dempsey in *The Golden Age of the Canadian Cowboy* (1995). He had his own Wild West shows as a side venture, but he ran the Stampede for 20 years after it began. He appeared in the annual parade in 1952 and passed away in 1953.

Guy Weadick and Florence LaDue (his wife), circa 1912

Herman Linder did *all* cowboys proud. Born in 1907 in Wisconsin, he was a proud member of the American National Cowboy Hall of Fame (1980) and the Canadian Rodeo Hall of Fame (1982), a recipient of the Order of Canada (1998), an honorary band chieftain of the Blood First Nation, a record-holding 22-time Calgary Stampede champion (including 12 All-Around titles), an entrepreneur and gentleman. He won both the Canadian Bronc and Bareback Bronc Riding championships during his first time at the Calgary Stampede. From 1929 to 1939 he was known as "King of the Cowboys" at the Stampede, winning the Canadian all-around championship seven times, and the North American championship five times in a row. His crowning achievement came when he practically won it all at the Calgary Stampede in 1934. He came in first on bareback, first on bulls, first on saddle broncs (Canadian entries) and second on saddle broncs (open entries). The stellar performance earned him North American and Canadian All-Around Cowboy recognition for that season. He died at age 95 at his ranch near Cardston, Alberta, in 2001.

Strawberry Rhubarb Streusel Pie

Many a farm and ranch in the West had a patch of strawberries and rhubarb in the garden, both of which were mainstays for cowboy desserts. Today rhubarb does not enjoy the same popularity that it once did. Many people have likely forgotten just how flavourful rhubarb is when sweetened with some strawberries and sugar, which mellow its natural tartness.

Chopped rhubarb	3 cups	750 mL
Sliced strawberries	1 cup	250 mL
Sugar	1 cup	250 mL
All-purpose flour	3 tbsp.	45 mL
Lemon juice	1/2 tsp.	2 mL
Unbaked 9 inch (23 cm) pie shell	1	1
All-purpose flour	2/3 cup	150 mL
Brown sugar, packed	1/2 cup	125 mL
Ground cinnamon	1/2 tsp.	2 mL
Cold butter (or hard margarine)	1/3 cup	75 mL

Combine rhubarb, strawberries, sugar, first amount of flour and lemon juice in a large bowl. Spread in pie shell.

Combine second amount of flour, brown sugar and cinnamon in a large bowl. Cut in butter until crumbly. Sprinkle over rhubarb mixture. Bake on bottom rack in 375°F (190°C) oven for about 50 minutes until golden. Serves 8.

1 serving: 370 Calories; 13 g Total Fat (4.5 g Mono, 1 g Poly, 7 g Sat); 20 mg Cholesterol; 61 g Carbohydrate (2 g Fibre, 41 g Sugar); 5 g Protein; 160 mg Sodium

Bumble Berry Pie

Most cowboys have a sweet tooth, no doubt because of a yearning for calories after a hard day's work on a farm or ranch, so a delicious bumble berry pie would certainly be a welcome dessert. Bumble berry pies are not too sweet, and their customary filling of at least three kinds of fresh berries has long been popular with country cooks. Of course, there's no such a thing as a "bumble berry"—we just like the term better than boring "mixed berry."

All-purpose flour	1 3/4 cups	425 mL
Brown sugar, packed	1 tbsp.	15 mL
Salt	3/4 tsp.	4 mL
Baking powder	1/4 tsp.	1 mL
Cold vegetable shortening	1/3 lb.	151 g
Cold water	3/4 cup	175 mL
White vinegar	2 tsp.	10 mL
Sugar	1 cup	250 mL
Lemon zest	1 tbsp.	15 mL
Corn starch	3 tbsp.	45 mL
Salt	1/2 tsp.	2 mL
Mixed berries (raspberries, blueberries, saskatoons, strawberries)	6 cups	1.5 L
Large egg, beaten	1	1

For the dough, combine first 4 ingredients in a large bowl. Cut in shortening until mixture resembles coarse crumbs.

Combine next 2 ingredients in a small bowl. Slowly add to flour mixture, stirring with a fork, until mixture starts to come together. You may not use all liquid. Do not over mix. Turn out onto work surface. Shape into 2 slightly flattened discs, one slightly larger than other. Wrap each with plastic wrap. Chill for 1 hour before rolling.

For the filling, in a large bowl combine sugar, lemon zest, corn starch and second amount of salt. Mix well so that there are no lumps. Add berries and stir to coat. Roll out larger dough portion on a lightly floured surface to about 1/8 inch (3 mm) thick. Line a 9 inch (23 cm) pie plate. Spread filling in pie shell. Roll out smaller portion of pastry on a lightly floured surface

(continued on next page)

to about 1/8 inch (3 mm) thick. Cut out several small vents with a small cookie cutter. Dampen edge of pastry shell in pie plate and cover with remaining pastry. Trim and crimp decorative edge to seal.

Brush crust with egg. Bake on bottom rack in 350°F (175°C) oven for 45 to 55 minutes until crust is golden and berries are tender. Serves 8.

1 serving: 420 Calories; 9 g Total Fat (2.5 g Mono, 0 g Poly, 5 g Sat); 55 mg Cholesterol; 83 g Carbohydrate (trace Fibre, 67 g Sugar); 3 g Protein; 160 mg Sodium

Raspberry Cobbler

Cobbler desserts go back to the days of the great cattle drives of the late 1800s, when peach cobbler was widely known as a cowboy favourite. A cobbler is a variation of pie that is baked in a deep dish or pan and has a fruit filling flavoured with sugar and spices. All manner of different fruits could be used for the filling— peaches, apricots, apples, pears, cherries, plums, blueberries, raspberries, blackberries and strawberries are popular choices. We've chosen raspberries for this recipe, but you could substitute another type of fruit, if you prefer.

Butter (or hard margarine), melted	1/4 cup	60 mL
All-purpose flour	1 cup	250 mL
Milk	3/4 cup	175 mL
Sugar	2 tbsp.	30 mL
Baking powder	2 tsp.	10 mL
Vanilla extract	1 tsp.	5 mL
Ground cinnamon	1/2 tsp.	2 mL
Ground nutmeg	1/4 tsp.	1 mL
Raspberries	2 cups	500 mL
Sugar	2 tbsp.	30 mL
Grated lemon zest	1 tsp.	5 mL
Water	1/2 cup	125 mL

Pour melted butter into bottom of a greased shallow baking dish. Set aside.

Combine next 7 ingredients in a medium bowl. Drop by tablespoons over butter.

Combine next 3 ingredients in a medium bowl. Sprinkle over flour mixture.

Drizzle with water. Do not stir. Bake in 350°F (175°C) oven for 40 to 45 minutes until bubbling and lightly browned. Serve warm. Serves 6.

1 serving: 220 Calories; 8 g Total Fat (2 g Mono, 0.5 g Poly, 5 g Sat); 20 mg Cholesterol; 31 g Carbohydrate (3 g Fibre, 12 g Sugar); 4 g Protein; 170 mg Sodium

Apple Bread Pudding

A good chuckwagon cook let nothing go to waste, and this apple bread pudding was a great way to use up day-old bread. Fresh fruit could be scarce on the trail, but the cook usually had an assortment of canned or dried fruits to choose from, dried apples being one of the most popular. Raisins would often be added to the dish as well, and perhaps caramel to sweeten the pudding. This is a great make-ahead dessert.

Apple juice	1/4 cup	60 mL
Chopped dried apple	1/2 cup	125 mL
Large eggs, fork beaten	2	2
Can of evaporated skim milk (13 1/2 oz., 385 mL)	1	1
Brown sugar	3 tbsp.	45 mL
Vanilla extract	1 tsp.	5 mL
Ground cinnamon	1/2 tsp.	2 mL
Ground nutmeg, to taste		
Whole grain bread slices, cubed	4	4
Brown sugar	4 tsp.	20 mL

Pour apple juice into a small saucepan and bring to a boil. Pour over dried apple in a small heatproof bowl. Let stand for 10 minutes until softened.

Combine eggs, evaporated milk, first amount of brown sugar, vanilla, cinnamon and nutmeg in a medium bowl. Stir in bread cubes and dried apple mixture. Spoon into 4 greased 1 cup (250 mL) ramekins.

Sprinkle with second amount of brown sugar. Place ramekins on a baking sheet with sides. Bake in 375°F (190°C) oven for about 20 minutes until top is golden and knife inserted in centre comes out clean. Let stand for 3 to 4 minutes until set. Serve warm. Serves 4.

1 serving: 350 Calories; 5 g Total Fat (1.5 g Mono, 1.5 g Poly, 11 g Sat); 105 mg Cholesterol; 65 g Carbohydrate (4 g Fibre, 41 g Sugar); 13 g Protein; 420 mg Sodium

Another popular dessert that dates back to the time of the cowboy is the Brown Betty. It is also a tasty way to use up day-old bread, but in this dish fresh apples are layered with bread crumbs and baked until the apples are soft and the bread crumbs are golden.

Burnt Sugar Cake

Most chuckwagon fare was basic, to say the least. The cook had limited space to store enough supplies to feed a group of cowboys for weeks on end and so relied on the staples—coffee, biscuits, beans and beef. Mealtimes could become a bit monotonous. One sure way for a cook to boost the morale of the group was to whip up a sweet dessert, and this cake would have been a perfect choice—no fancy ingredients necessary! A syrup made of caramelized (not burnt) sugar in both the cake and the icing imparts a rich caramel-like flavour.

Sugar	2 cups	500 mL
Water	1 cup	250 mL
Butter, softened	1/2 cup	125 mL
Sugar	1 cup	250 mL
Large eggs	2	2
Vanilla extract	1 tsp.	5 mL
All-purpose flour	2 cups	500 mL
Baking powder	2 tsp.	10 mL
Salt	1/4 tsp.	1 mL
Water	1 cup	250 mL
Icing (confectioner's) sugar	2 cups	500 mL
Butter	1/4 cup	60 mL
Milk	1 tbsp.	15 mL
Vanilla extract	1 tsp.	5 mL

For the burnt sugar syrup, heat first amount of sugar in a large heavy frying pan over medium-low. Stir often as it melts. Remove from heat when it becomes a dark butterscotch colour. Carefully add 1/4 cup (60 mL) of water. It will sputter furiously. Stir, then pour in 3/4 cup (175 mL) of water. Return pan to heat and stir until dissolves. Set aside to cool.

For the cake, cream first amount of butter and second amount of sugar in a large bowl. Beat in eggs, one at a time. Stir in fist amount of vanilla.

Combine flour, baking powder and salt in a medium bowl.

Mix 1/3 cup (75 mL) burnt sugar syrup with second amount of water. Add to butter mixture in 2 parts alternately with flour mixture in 3 parts, beginning and ending with flour mixture. Divide batter between 2 greased 8 inch (20 cm) round layer pans. Bake in 350°F (175°C) oven for 30 to 35 minutes until a toothpick inserted in middle comes out clean. Set aside to cool.

(continued on next page)

For the icing, beat icing sugar, second amount of butter, 2 tbsp. (30 mL) burnt sugar syrup, milk and second amount of vanilla in a large bowl until smooth, adding more milk or icing sugar as necessary. Spread over cake. Serves 12.

1 serving: 420 Calories; 9 g Total Fat (2.5 g Mono, 0 g Poly, 5 g Sat); 55 mg Cholesterol; 83 g Carbohydrate (trace Fibre, 67 g Sugar); 3 g Protein; 160 mg Sodium

Old-time Pound Cake

A pound cake is an old-fashioned cake traditionally made with a pound of each of four key ingredients: flour, butter, eggs and sugar. Today not all recipes call for a pound of butter thanks to our diet-conscious society. This is an easy cake to make, and many a camp cook would add some berries, chocolate chips or lemon to the mix.

Eggs, separated, at room temperature	10	10
Butter (or hard margarine), softened	2 cups	500 mL
Sugar	2 cups	500 mL
Baking soda	1/2 tsp.	2 mL
Water	1 tsp.	5 mL
Lemon flavouring	1 tsp.	5 mL
All-purpose flour	4 cups	1 L
Cream of tartar	1 tsp.	5 mL

Beat egg whites in a large bowl until stiff. Set aside.

Cream butter and sugar together in a large mixing bowl. Add egg yolks and beat well, then fold in egg whites.

Dissolve baking soda in water, and add lemon flavouring. Fold into mixture.

Combine flour and cream of tartar. Sift half of flour over batter and fold in. Repeat with second half of flour. Turn into a foil-lined loaf pan and bake in 300°F (150°C) oven for about 2 hours until a toothpick inserted in centre comes out clean. Serves 16.

1 serving: 430 Calories; 23 g Total Fat (6 g Mono, 1 g Poly, 15 g Sat); 60 mg Cholesterol; 49 g Carbohydrate (trace Fibre, 25 g Sugar); 6 g Protein; 240 mg Sodium

A chuckwagon cook who did not have access to eggs, milk and butter would sometimes whip up cowboy cake to treat his crew to something sweet. This cake was egg and dairy free, relying on bacon grease for its fat. A similar cake, called depression cake, was popular during the Great Depression, when eggs, milk and butter were scarce or prohibitively expensive.

Matrimonial Cake

Matrimonial cake is a uniquely western Canadian name for the dessert more commonly known as date squares. These squares date back at least as far as the early days of settlement in the Canadian West, though some authorities claim the squares go back to the days of the Roman Empire. The name "matrimonial cake" is said to refer to the texture of the squares—the smooth filling and rough base and topping reflect the contrast between the easy and difficult times of marriage. Don't skimp on the butter to get this recipe right!

Rolled oats	1 1/2 cups	375 mL
All-purpose flour	1 1/4 cups	300 mL
Brown sugar, packed	1 cup	250 mL
Baking soda	1 tsp.	5 mL
Salt	1/2 tsp.	2 mL
Butter (or hard margarine)	1 cup	250 mL
Chopped dates	1 1/2 cups	375 mL
Water	2/3 cup	150 mL
Sugar	1/2 cup	125 mL

Combine first 5 ingredients in a large bowl. Cut in butter until mixture resembles very coarse crumbs. Press slightly more than half of mixture firmly in greased 9 x 9 inch (23 x 23 cm) pan. Set remaining mixture aside.

Combine dates, water and sugar in a medium saucepan. Bring to a boil over medium heat. Reduce heat to medium-low. Simmer, uncovered, for about 10 minutes until dates are softened and water is almost absorbed, adding more water if necessary while simmering to soften dates. Spread evenly over bottom layer of crumbs. Sprinkle remaining crumb mixture evenly over top. Press down lightly. Bake in 350°F (175°C) oven for about 30 minutes until golden. Let stand in pan on wire rack until cool. Serves 36.

1 serving: 130 Calories; 5 g Total Fat (1.5 g Mono, 0 g Poly, 3.5 g Sat); 15 mg Cholesterol; 20 g Carbohydrate (trace Fibre, 13 g Sugar); 1 g Protein; 105 mg Sodium

INDEX